The Lean Mindset

The Lean Mindset
Ask the Right Questions

Mary Poppendieck and Tom Poppendieck

♦♦Addison-Wesley

Upper Saddle River, NJ • Boston • Indianapolis • San Francisco
New York • Toronto • Montreal • London • Munich • Paris • Madrid
Capetown • Sydney • Tokyo • Singapore • Mexico City

Many of the designations used by manufacturers and sellers to distinguish their products are claimed as trademarks. Where those designations appear in this book, and the publisher was aware of a trademark claim, the designations have been printed with initial capital letters or in all capitals.

The authors and publisher have taken care in the preparation of this book, but make no expressed or implied warranty of any kind and assume no responsibility for errors or omissions. No liability is assumed for incidental or consequential damages in connection with or arising out of the use of the information or programs contained herein.

The publisher offers excellent discounts on this book when ordered in quantity for bulk purchases or special sales, which may include electronic versions and/or custom covers and content particular to your business, training goals, marketing focus, and branding interests. For more information, please contact:

U.S. Corporate and Government Sales
(800) 382-3419
corpsales@pearsontechgroup.com

For sales outside the United States, please contact:

International Sales
international@pearsoned.com

Visit us on the Web: informit.com/aw

Library of Congress Cataloging-in-Publication Data

Poppendieck, Mary (Mary B.)
  The lean mindset : ask the right questions/Mary Poppendieck, Tom Poppendieck.
    pages   cm
  Includes bibliographical references and index.
  ISBN 978-0-321-89690-2 (pbk. : alk. paper)
  1. Organizational effectiveness. 2. Management. 3. Cost control.
  4. Lean manufacturing. I. Poppendieck, Thomas David. II. Title.
  HD58.9.P67 2014
  658.4'013--dc23   2013030856

ISBN-13: 978-0-321-89690-2
ISBN-10:   0-321-89690-4
Text printed in the United States on recycled paper at Courier in Westford, Massachusetts.
First printing, September 2013

Contents

Preface

Several years ago, Henrik Kniberg invited us to stop in Stockholm and give a talk. He met us at the train station, helped roll our suitcases to a nearby hotel, and invited us to the small office he shared with other consultants at Crisp. There, he presented us with a book he had recently finished, *Scrum and XP from the Trenches,* the story of one of his early forays into agile software development. We were impressed.

Henrik has invited us back to Stockholm many times, where we partnered in offering Deep Lean events, Leading Lean workshops, and many community talks. We have joined Henrik and his family for fishing in the Stockholm archipelago, canoeing on Lake Mälaren, and many barbecues at their lakefront home. We even met in New Zealand when both of our families decided to spend Christmas there.

Henrik's clear thinking and innovative applications of lean can be found in his book *Lean from the Trenches* and in his blog.[1] We love the way Henrik illustrates his work with engaging sketches that simplify and clarify complex concepts. In fact, our book was starting to look a bit bland by comparison. So we asked Henrik if he would contribute some sketches to liven things up. We are sure you will enjoy the results: characters scattered liberally throughout the book and diagrams that are worth a thousand words. For an additional treat, enjoy Henrik's well-illustrated account, at the end of Chapter 4, of how Spotify develops products.

Thank you, Henrik! Your contributions have truly enhanced this book.

---

1. blog.crisp.se/author/henrikkniberg.

Our sincere thanks also go to Theresa Smith and Thad Scheer, whose company, Sphere of Influence, transformed itself into a software design studio. Theresa's story of their journey from Agile to Design can be found in Chapter 3.

We are very grateful to Patrick Elwer and Tim Gallagher from Intel's Product Development Engineering group in Portland, Oregon, who helped us tell the story of their continuing journey to keep up with Moore's Law. Many thanks to Mats Lindén, Hendrik Esser, Ulf Hansson, and Micael Caiman for sharing the Ericsson approach to meeting serious market challenges in the telecommunications industry. We are deeply indebted to Eric Presley, CTO of CareerBuilder, who shared his company's story. Many thanks to FINN.no CEO Christian Printzell Halvorsen, who gave us a rare glimpse of a company dealing successfully with disruptive technologies. Last, but not least, we thank Joe Justice for telling us the WIKISPEED story and sharing his philosophy for working with volunteers.

One of the things that make a book great is the time and effort of reviewers who wade through early drafts and make suggestions for improvement. A special thanks to members of the Agile Austin Book Club for reviewing the book and to Jay Paulson for consolidating the group's feedback. We also thank Michael Abugow, Gojko Adzic, Christian Beck, Samuel Crescêncio, Mike Dwyer, James Grenning, Jez Humble, Carsten Ruseng Jakobsen, Tomo Lennox, Julien Mazloum, Matthew McCullough, Lee Nicholls, Linda Rising, and Bas Vodde for their insightful comments.

Finally, we truly appreciate the guidance of our editor, Greg Doench, and the contributions made by Elizabeth Ryan, production editor; Barbara Wood, copy editor; and Dick Evans, indexer. Thanks again to the great team from Addison-Wesley!

Mary and Tom Poppendieck
July 2013

About the Authors

Mary Poppendieck has led teams implementing various business solutions, ranging from enterprise supply chain management to digital media. Mary is the president of Poppendieck.LLC, which specializes in bringing lean techniques to software development.

Tom Poppendieck, an enterprise analyst, architect, and agile process mentor at Poppendieck.LLC, currently assists organizations in applying lean principles and tools to software development processes.

The Poppendiecks are authors of *Lean Software Development,* winner of the 2004 Jolt Software Development Productivity Award, *Implementing Lean Software Development,* and *Leading Lean Software Development* (all from Addison-Wesley).

Introduction

Back in the 1990s, when open source was an outlier and eBay was a startup, most people believed that economic transactions—at least important ones—required a trustworthy company to back them up. And trustworthy companies required a management structure to make sure that important work got done.

When economists first stumbled upon Linux, their instinctive reaction was "This is impossible!"[1] How can a deeply complex operating system that was developed and maintained by volunteers be reliable enough for widespread adoption by businesses? But today Linux, along with GNU, is arguably the most successful operating system in the world. Apache HTTP Server has powered over 60% of all Web servers since 2000. Sendmail and its commercial derivatives deliver 65% of e-mail worldwide. All this was accomplished without traditional management structures or work practices.

eBay faced a different dilemma; it needed to find a way to create trust between buyers and sellers who were strangers. The company devised a review and ranking system that quickly exposed bad behavior. This widely imitated reputation system has kept instances of fraud in consumer-to-consumer transactions amazingly low, paving the path for a broad range of trust-based businesses.

While the Internet was growing up, it was used mostly by scientists. They developed it into a tool to support the way they worked; it helped

---

1. See Peter Kollock, "The Economies of Online Cooperation: Gifts and Public Goods in Cyberspace," Chapter 9 of *Communities in Cyberspace*, ed. Marc A. Smith and Peter Kollock, pp. 219–40 (Routledge, 1999).

them find information, share knowledge, collaborate with peers, and establish a reputation. By the time the Web became available for commercial use in the mid-1990s, it was a well-developed research tool, and its capabilities nudged newcomers toward the same work practices that scientists used. So it should be no surprise that early users of the commercial Internet tended to favor the academic model of working, which is light on management but strong on guidance by a master in the field; light on efficiency and strong on experimentation; light on proprietary knowledge while strongly encouraging information sharing and collaboration across disciplines.

Early Internet users included many software developers, who were comfortable with the primitive user interfaces available at the time. A group of developers used the Internet as a collaboration platform to spawn a movement aimed at changing the work practices commonly used in software development. They lobbied for a customer-focused, team-based, experimental approach to their work, mirroring the academic practices already supported by the Internet. Over time these agile development practices gained widespread acceptance and emerged as a credible—even superior—approach to developing software-intensive products. It turns out that the academic approach to learning works quite well for creating innovative new products and services.

The arc of change toward collaborative work practices[2] has followed the growing sophistication and accessibility of Web-based tools that support knowledge sharing and collaboration. Consider Karen, our oldest granddaughter, who is about to head off to college. She is perhaps the quintessential digital native: proficient at surfing the Internet before she was ten, posting her thoughts on Facebook by 12, engaged in a stream of text messages for several years. It won't be long before Karen and her cohorts will be the only kind of college graduates available to fill the jobs that our organizations create.

Digital natives have been immersed in an environment of readily available knowledge and instant access to colleagues for as long as they can remember. They know how to leverage the advantages of this environment, and they will expect to find it in their workplace. They will expect easy, transparent access to information; they will expect to collaborate with a wide range of people; they will expect anywhere,

---

2. We first heard of this Arc of Change from Yochai Benkler of Harvard Law School in his keynote talk at Lean Software and Systems 2012, Boston, May 16, 2012. See also Yochai Benkler, "The Unselfish Gene," *Harvard Business Review*, July–August 2011.

anytime access to their network of peers; they will probably not make much distinction between work and personal activities; they will certainly expect to be trusted.

Of course, organizations should not blindly cater to the expectations of the new kids in the company. But it turns out that the academic approach to working is a good model for bringing out the best in knowledge workers of all ages. The kids are on to something that works really well—for everyone.

This is a book about the design, development, and delivery of exceptional products and services. Therefore, it is a book about creating work environments where Karen and her colleagues routinely leverage a growing body of knowledge and multiple perspectives to create and launch brilliant products and services. It is a book about learning: learning about customers and creating experiences they love. It is about discovering effective ways to develop and deliver those experiences. Finally, this is a book about gaining the insight and adaptability to thrive in a rapidly changing world.

Lean Is a Mindset

Lean is a mindset—a mental model of how the world works. In this book we present a mental model of how to design and deliver amazing products that delight customers. We start with two foundational questions: *What is the purpose of a business? What kind of work systems are best for accomplishing that purpose?* Next we explore ways to create an environment that energizes the people whose intelligence and creativity are essential to creating great products. Then we turn our attention to the process of creating products and services that work well and delight customers. We move on to consider efficiency—because this is a book about lean, after all, and lean has always been associated with efficiency. We demonstrate that genuine efficiency in product development is about developing the right product, creating a steady flow of new knowledge, and linking the design and delivery processes together to gain rapid customer feedback. Finally, we move beyond efficiency to innovation and discuss how great products come from changing the focus . . . from productivity to impact . . . from predictability to experimentation . . . from efficiency to decentralization . . . and from product to problem.

Through research results and case studies, the book builds a mental model of how lean design and development should look and feel in order to foster a lean mindset in organizations that create products and services. The case studies in the book are not to be emulated so much as absorbed, because developing a mindset is not about copying practices—it's about developing the expertise to ask the right questions, solve the right problems, and do the right thing in the situation at hand.

How Mindsets Work

Our minds are amazing. It appears to us that we make decisions thoughtfully and deliberately, but research has shown that most of the time we make decisions instinctively, based on the mindset we have developed over time. It's almost as if we have two minds—one that builds our mindset and corrects it from time to time, and another that reacts quickly to situations as they develop, drawing on the currently available mindset to arbitrate trade-offs.

The idea that we have two rather different decision-making processes is not a new one; the literature is filled with many varied descriptions of our two minds. One mind might be intuitive, the other analytical; one mind could be emotional, the other rational; one reflexive, the other reflective. One mind might look for patterns, the other follows rules; one mind acts on tacit knowledge, the other prefers explicit information; one mind makes snap decisions, the other takes time to think things through.

Psychologists Keith Stanovich and Richard West proposed that we take all of these different theories about people being of two minds and combine them into a single theory: the **Dual Processing Theory**.[3] The theory works something like this: Humans have two different methods for processing information, and each method operates more or less independently of the other one, exchanging information at appropriate times. Sometimes the two processes arrive at different conclusions, and that's when we become aware of the fact that we have two minds, because they are in conflict with each other.

In order to avoid a bias toward any particular way of describing our two "minds," Stanovich and West proposed that we simply call them **System 1** and **System 2**.

---

3. See K. E. Stanovich, *Who Is Rational? Studies of Individual Differences in Reasoning* (Lawrence Elrbaum Associates, 1999); and K. E. Stanovich and R. F. West, "Individual Differences in Reasoning: Implications for the Rationality Debate," *Behav. Brain Sci.* 2000 (23): 645–726.

System 1 and System 2

An excellent description of System 1 and System 2 can be found in Nobel laureate Daniel Kahneman's book *Thinking, Fast and Slow*.[4] Kahneman describes System 1 as our fast-thinking self, the one that makes decisions based on intuition, is influenced by emotions, uses tacit knowledge, and operates out of habit. If you have ever walked into your home after a long day at work and wondered how you got there, you can be sure that System 1 brought you home all by itself while you were distracted with other things. For getting the everyday things in life done, we can't beat System 1; we might think of it as our autopilot mode.

System 2 is the part of us that analyzes situations, considers alternatives, plans for the future, and does the math. Whenever we find ourselves pausing to consider something carefully, it's like switching from autopilot to manual mode; our analytical mind takes over from our intuition and works out rational choices. Although System 2 is not actively directing us most of the time, it regularly checks up on System 1 to see if it needs to intervene. When we develop a decision tree to make sure we consider all of the alternatives before making a decision, System 2 is in charge. When we are quiet and polite even though we are angry, System 2 is keeping System 1 in check.

Generally speaking, we operate in autopilot mode. If unusual circumstances arise, we switch out of autopilot and over to manual mode. And it is in this manual mode that we develop or modify our mindsets. We will need to spend a good amount of time in manual mode, with System 2 fully engaged, in order to change an established mindset. But there's a problem: System 2 is slow. It takes much longer than System 1 to make decisions and get things done. In addition, System 2 is lazy; its preferred approach is to turn as much work as possible over to System 1. So modifying a mindset takes deliberate effort and considerable time—time spent reading a book, for example.

We would like to introduce you to Otto and Anna:

 Otto represents our System 1 mind, so he is on autopilot much of the time. He is intuitive and moves easily, adjusting rapidly to whatever happens. He has a lot of

4. Daniel Kahneman, *Thinking, Fast and Slow* (Farrar, Straus and Giroux, 2011).

experience in his specialty area and is comfortable trusting his expertise and intuition to guide his actions.

 Anna represents our System 2 mind; she analyzes situations before she acts. She knows that the best decisions are those based on evidence. She is good at gathering data, running experiments, and weighing the impact of various choices before making a decision.

Otto and Anna are very opinionated. They will be reading this book along with you, and they will ask questions and challenge our ideas on a regular basis. We put our dialog with Otto and Anna in a sidebar so you can follow along with your favorite co-reader.

The Fabric of Lean

Lean principles are woven throughout this book, just as they must be woven throughout the fabric of an organization with a lean mindset.

Chapter 1: The Purpose of Business emphasizes the principle *Optimize the Whole*, taking the Shareholder Value Theory to task for the short-term thinking it produces. The alternative is to *Focus on Customers*, whose loyalty determines the long-term success of any business. It is one thing for business leaders to have a vision of who their customers are, but quite another to put the work systems in place to serve those customers well. In the end, the front-line workers in a company are the ones who make or break the customer experience.

It turns out that the "rational" thinking behind the Shareholder Value Theory has had a strong influence on the way workers are treated. It all boils down to Douglas McGregor's Theory X and Theory Y. Theory X assumes that people don't like work and will do as little as possible. Theory Y assumes the opposite: Most people are eager to work and want to do a good job. The lean principle *Energize Workers* is solidly based on Theory Y—start with the assumption that workers care about their company and their customers, and this will be a self-fulfilling prophecy. The principle of reciprocity is at work here—if you treat workers well, they will treat customers well, and customers will reward the company with their business.

Reciprocity was the basis of human cooperation long before money was invented, and it remains central to human behavior today. However, reciprocity is local. It depends on group (or team) size, team member engagement, and norms for creating and enforcing mutual obligations. When designing work systems that *Energize Workers* and help them *Focus on Customers*, leverage the power of peers, rather than incentives, to steer behavior in the right direction.

Chapter 2: Energized Workers is based on the work of Mihaly Csikszentmihalyi, who found that the most energizing human experience is pursuing a well-framed challenge. Energized workers have a purpose that is larger than the company and a direct line of sight between their effort and achieving that purpose. They strive to reach their full potential through challenging work that requires increasing skill and expertise. They thrive on the right kind of challenge—a challenge that is not so easy as to be boring and not so hard as to be discouraging, a challenge that appeals to aspirations or to duty, depending on the "regulatory fit."

Regulatory fit is a theory that says some people (and some companies—startups, for example) are biased toward action and experimentation and respond well to aspirational challenges. Other people (and companies—big ones, for example) prefer to be safe rather than sorry. For them, challenges that focus on duty and failure prevention are more inspiring. But either way, a challenge that is well matched to the people and the situation is one of the best ways to energize workers.

One of the most important challenges in a lean environment is to *Constantly Improve*. Whether it is a long-term journey to improve product development practices or an ongoing fault injection practice to hone emergency response skills, striving to constantly get better engages teams and brings out the best in people.

Chapter 3: Delighted Customers urges readers to *Focus on Customers*, understand what they really need, and make sure that the right products and services are developed. This is the first step in the quest to *Eliminate Waste*, especially in software development, where building the wrong thing is the biggest waste of all.

Some products present extraordinary technical challenges—inventing the airplane or finding wicked problems in a large data management system. Other products need insightful design in order to really solve customer problems. Before diving into development, it is important to *Learn First* to understand the essential system issues and customer problems before attempting to solve them.

When developing a product, it is important to look beyond what customers ask for, because working from a list of requirements is not likely to create products that customers *love*. Instead, leaders like GE

Healthcare's Doug Dietz, who saw a terrified child approach his MRI scanner, understand that a product is not finished until the customer experience is as well designed as the hardware and software.

Great products are designed by teams that are able to empathize with customers, ask the right questions, identify critical problems, examine multiple possibilities, and then develop products and services that delight customers.

Chapter 4: Genuine Efficiency starts by emphasizing that authentic, sustainable efficiency does *not* mean layoffs, low costs, and controlling work systems. Development is only a small portion of a product's life cycle, but it has a massive influence on the product's success. It is folly to cut corners in development only to end up with costly or underperforming products in the end. Those who *Optimize the Whole* understand that in product development, efficiency is first and foremost about building the right thing.

Two case studies from Ericsson Networks demonstrate that small batches, rapid flow, autonomous feature teams, and pull from the market can dramatically increase both predictability and time to market on large products. Here we see the lean principles of *Focus on Customers*, *Deliver Fast*, *Energize Workers*, and *Build Quality In* at work.

A case study from CareerBuilder further emphasizes how focusing on the principle of *Deliver Fast* leads to every other lean principle, especially *Build Quality In* and *Focus on Customers*. A look at Lean Startup techniques shows that constant experiments by the product team can rapidly refine the business model for a new product as well as uncover its most important features. Here the lean principles of *Optimize the Whole*, *Deliver Fast*, and *Keep Getting Better* are particularly apparent.

Finally, a discussion of how Spotify develops products summarizes most of the lean principles one more time, with a particular emphasis on customer focus, data-driven experiments, empowered teams, and rapid feedback.

Chapter 5: Breakthrough Innovation starts with a cautionary tale about how vulnerable businesses are—even simple businesses like newspapers can lose their major source of revenue seemingly overnight. But disruptive technologies don't usually change things quite that fast; threatened companies are usually blind to the threat until it's too late. How can it be that industry after industry is overrun with disruptive innovation and incumbent companies are unable to respond?

The problem, it seems, is too much focus on today's operations—maybe even too much focus on the lean principle of *Eliminate Waste*—and not enough focus on the bigger picture, on *Optimize the Whole*. Too much focus on adding features for today's customers and not enough focus on potential customers who need lower prices and fewer features. Too much focus on predictability and not enough focus on experimentation. Too much focus on productivity and not enough focus on impact. Too much focus on the efficiency of centralization and not enough appreciation for the resiliency of decentralization.

Lean organizations appreciate that the real knowledge resides at the place where work is done, in the teams that develop the products, in the customers who are struggling with problems. Several case studies—including Harman, Intuit, and GE Healthcare—show how the lean principles of *Focus on Customers, Energize Workers, Learn First,* and *Deliver Fast* help companies develop breakthrough innovations before they get blindsided by someone else's disruptive innovations.

Developing a lean mindset is a process that takes time and deliberate practice, just like developing any other kind of expertise. No matter how well you "know" the ideas presented in this book, actually using them in your work on a day-to-day basis requires that you spend time trying the ideas out, experimenting with them, making mistakes, and learning.

Cultivating a lean mindset—especially in an organization—is a continuing journey. We hope this book brings you another step along the path.

1

The Purpose of Business

The Rise of Rational Economics

In 1950, as George Merck retired from his job as president of pharmaceutical giant Merck & Co., he summarized the underlying philosophy that drove its success:

> We try never to forget that medicine is for the patient. It is not for profits. The profits follow; and if we have remembered this, they have never failed to appear. The better we have remembered it, the larger they have been.[1]

The idea that the purpose of business is to serve customers was widely accepted at the time. The Second World War had recently ended, and the homecoming of untold numbers of soldiers triggered a boom in births as well as in business. After years of austerity, demand was particularly high, and businesses were eager to supply new products to a growing population. The economy had nowhere to go but up.

But if we fast-forward 25 years to 1975, we find that business opportunities were not so plentiful anymore. The war generation was retiring, and a new cohort of business leaders was faced with slower growth, broader competition, and limited memories of depression and war-era hard times. The conventional wisdom that companies should preserve cash and take care of their employees was feeling a bit outdated to this new generation of business leaders.

---

1. Jim Collins and Jerry I. Porras, *Built to Last: Successful Habits of Visionary Companies* (Harper Business, 2004), p. 48.

In 1974 Peter Drucker, a leading management thinker of the twentieth century, published his seminal book on management.[2] He wrote that **the purpose of business is to create a customer**—to discover a customer need and find a way to satisfy that need. However, managers were struggling with companies that had grown large and complex and were experiencing stagnant growth. They were certainly trying to create new customers, but it was difficult.

About this time an attractive new idea appeared on the scene—one that seemed a bit more actionable and better suited to the slowing economy. The idea was based on the proposition that professional managers are agents of the owners (shareholders) of a firm.[3] As agents, managers make decisions for the owners, but like all agents, they are probably utility maximizers (interested in maximizing their own personal gain). Therefore, there's a good chance that a company's top managers will work to further their own interests at the expense of shareholder interests. One way to guard against this conflict of interest is to hold top managers accountable for making sure that shareholders receive the best possible return on their investment. The new theory could be stated simply: **The purpose of business is to maximize shareholder value.**

 At the time there was widespread faith in the intelligence and efficiency of markets, which made the Shareholder Value Theory look very attractive.[4] Letting the market decide whether or not a CEO was doing a good job seemed like an obvious way to ensure that the best interests of a company were being served by its leader.

It is impossible to understate the influence of the Shareholder Value Theory on business practices, especially in the United States. In order to increase shareholder value (or its proxy, share prices), companies shifted from "retain and reinvest" strategies to "downsize and distribute" strategies.[5] Instead of investing in people and research, companies outsourced

2. Peter Drucker, *Management: Tasks, Responsibilities, Practices* (Harper & Row, 1974).

3. Michael C. Jensen and William H. Meckling, "Theory of the Firm: Managerial Behavior, Agency Costs and Ownership Structure," *Journal of Financial Economics*, October 1976.

4. Jeffrey Pfeffer, "Shareholders First? Not So Fast . . . ," *Harvard Business Review*, August 2009.

5. Justin Fox and Jay W. Lorsch, "What Good Are Shareholders?" *Harvard Business Review*, July–August 2012.

jobs and distributed profits to shareholders. To keep CEOs properly focused, their compensation was increasingly tied to share price.

These strategies increased profits in the short run, but companies struggled over the long term. Not only did a vast number of jobs disappear, but the skill embedded in those jobs also disappeared. Within a decade of outsourcing manufacturing, companies found they could no longer engineer complex technical products and scale them up, so engineering jobs disappeared as well.[6] Of course, costs were lower, but over time innovation stalled, sales flattened, and share prices faltered.

Did the Shareholder Value Theory work in practice? The short answer is: Probably not. Roger Martin of the University of Toronto points out that the rate of return on shareholder investments has not improved since 1976—if anything it has declined.[7]

But the theory worked pretty well for CEOs, especially in the United States. In 1976 U.S. CEO income was 36 times that of an average worker; in 1993 it was 131 times higher; by 2010, CEOs in the United States made 369 times more than the average worker.[8]

Rosabeth Moss Kanter of the Harvard Business School has spent years studying truly successful companies and how they think. She sums up her findings this way:

> Traditionally, economists and financiers have argued that the sole purpose of business is to make money—the more the better. That conveniently narrow image, deeply embedded in the American capitalist system, molds the actions of most corporations, constraining them to focus on maximizing short-term profits and delivering returns to shareholders. . . .
>
> Rather than viewing organizational processes as ways of extracting more economic value, great companies create frameworks that use societal value and human values as decision-making criteria. They believe that corporations have a purpose and meet stakeholders' needs in many ways: by producing goods and services that improve the lives of users; by providing jobs and

---

6. Andy Grove, "Andy Grove: How America Can Create Jobs," *Bloomburg Business Week,* July 1, 2010.

7. Roger Martin (Dean of the Rotman School of Management, University of Toronto), "The Age of Customer Capitalism," *Harvard Business Review,* January–February 2010.

8. Dan Ariely, *Predictably Irrational: The Hidden Forces That Shape Our Decisions* (HarperCollins, 2010), p. 17.

enhancing workers' quality of life; by developing a strong network of suppliers and business partners; and by ensuring financial viability, which provides resources for improvements, innovations, and returns to investors.[9]

> **Anna:** Why not focus on maximizing *long-term* shareholder value?
>
> **M&T [Mary and Tom]:** In an interview in 2009, Jack Welch said, "On the face of it, shareholder value is the dumbest idea in the world. Shareholder value is a result, not a strategy . . . your main constituencies are your employees, your customers and your products."[10] In other words, the best approach is not to worry about shareholder value at all, but to focus on creating energized workers, delighted customers, and breakthrough innovation. When done right, this will result in increased shareholder value over time.

The Tech Generation

Fast-forward another quarter century to the year 2000, and we find a new generation of tech-savvy leaders whose companies have set the rules about how we search, shop, connect with friends, and carry the Internet in our pockets. They don't feel the need to follow the norms of the last century. Instead they have rediscovered something that we used to know: **Purpose is the master and profit is the servant.**

Take a look at the things that fast-growing Internet companies focus on: They are obsessed with providing great experiences to their consumers and communities. They concentrate on creating a culture in which talented employees are passionate about their work and engaged in delivering exceptional value. These companies state clearly in their IPO documents that they do not intend to focus on making money for shareholders.

Amazon.com, for instance, warns its investors that it plans to make decisions for the long term, so investors looking for short-term profits should look elsewhere. Its strategy is to focus relentlessly on custom-

---

9. Rosabeth Moss Kanter, "How Great Companies Think Differently," *Harvard Business Review*, November 2011. Used with permission.
10. *Financial Times*, "Welch Condemns Share Price Focus," March 12, 2009, www.ft.com/intl/cms/s/0/294ff1f2-0f27-11de-ba10-0000779fd2ac.html#axzz2EyBD8eJ2.

ers, hire talented employees, and take serious risks—some of which can be expected to fail.[11]

Google also warns potential shareholders that it will adopt a long-term focus on accomplishing its mission, which is to organize the world's information and make it universally accessible and useful.[12] Eric Schmidt of Google commented:

> Apple proves that if you organize around the consumer, the rest of it will follow. That's something that I did not understand until Google. Google runs in a similar way. Try to figure out how to solve the consumer problem, and then the revenue will show up.[13]

Facebook says in its IPO document: "Simply put: we don't build services to make money; we make money to build better services."

Otto: What did Peter Drucker mean when he said the purpose of business is to create a customer? How do you create customers?

M&T: Drucker recommended that business leaders start with the question *What business are we in?* The way to answer this question is by asking another question: *Who are our customers?* That is a critical question, and it is never easy to answer. But once a company decides whom it should serve, it must develop a deep understanding of the lives, the needs, the realities, and the values of those customers. Then it must implement innovative work systems so its employees can fill those customer needs by delivering the products and services that customers will find valuable.[14]

Case: Who Are Our Customers?

Todd Park graduated from Harvard College with a degree in economics and joined Booz Allen Hamilton's managed care strategy practice, where he met Jonathan S. Bush. The pair decided that they were entrepreneurs at heart, so in 1997 they started up a maternity care business—Athenahealth. They were sure they knew how to provide

---

11. http://phx.corporate-ir.net/phoenix.zhtml?c=97664&p=irol-govHighlights.
12. http://investor.google.com/corporate/2004/ipo-founders-letter.html.
13. Marc Benioff and Eric Schmidt at Dreamforce 2011, September 5, 2011, www.youtube.com/watch?v=JDl5hb0XbfY.
14. Drucker, *Management.*

better care for less money. To say the company got off to a slow start would be a vast understatement. The two health care consultants discovered that their business acumen wasn't as good as they thought it was, and they struggled with the intricacies of running a medical clinic.

Over time Park and Bush learned what it took to run a successful health care business. Then they began to ask themselves who their real customers should be and what those customers needed. As they wrestled with their clinic's information systems, they realized that their customers should be people like themselves—people running a health care business. They knew from personal experience exactly what those customers needed, so they morphed Athenahealth from a maternity clinic into an Internet-based medical practice management business. The partners found a ready market for their new offering, and the company grew rapidly. A decade of intense effort was rewarded with a hugely successful IPO in 2007.[15]

Act II: What Business Are We In?

At 35, Todd Park decided he had plenty of money to retire, spend more time at home, and start a family. He left the company in the hands of Jonathan Bush and moved from Boston to California. But less than two years later, as Park was enjoying his spare time with an infant crawling underfoot, he got a call from Bill Corr, the Deputy Secretary of the U.S. Department of Health and Human Services (HHS). Corr asked Park to join HHS as Entrepreneur in Residence. A government job was the last thing Park needed, and moving to Washington, DC, was the last thing his wife was interested in. There was no economic reason for Park to place his assets in a blind trust and move his reluctant family back east, but he was strongly tempted by the purpose of HHS: *Improve the health, safety, and well-being of America.* Eventually he accepted the job and dove into it like a man on a mission; it was as if he wanted to hurry up and make HHS entrepreneurial so he could get back to retirement.

If Todd Park had learned one thing at Athenahealth, it was to start with the question *What business are we in?* As a self-proclaimed "data guy," Park was tremendously impressed at the wealth of data in HHS databases; he could just imagine how useful this data might be if it were publicly available. Fortunately, there was a precedent for releasing government data to the public. Decades ago the National Oceanic

---

15. Athenahealth was valued "north of a billion dollars" after its IPO in 2007.

and Atmospheric Administration (NOAA) decided to make its data broadly and easily accessible, forming the basis of numerous weather reporting and tracking businesses. Park thought this was a great model to follow; he decided that HHS should get into the business of making its databases publicly available. He set out to create an HHS data platform upon which innovators could build applications.

Park's job was to bring a startup mentality to the huge HHS bureaucracy. Thinking back on his entrepreneurial days, he recalled: "There was one characteristic that consistently differentiated the best entrepreneurs, the best entrepreneurial team members, from the average ones. And it was that they were not in it for the stock options. They weren't in it for the fame. They were in it because they couldn't stand the idea of a world not having what they were building. It was this profound *mission orientation* to deliver something that was helpful."[16]

So how does one bring mission orientation to a bureaucracy? It turns out it was not as difficult as you might think. Park found that there were many dedicated, mission-oriented people at HHS, eager to work on projects that would improve the health, safety, and well-being of America. "The idea is to find a particular idea or initiative that would be good to get going," Todd Park says. "The first thing that I do is I find the three to five people at HHS who had that idea a long time ago, who have been obsessing about it, who know a lot more about it than I do, who have connections and data and resources and people that they can throw in the mix. And then I recruit them to join a virtual startup to do this thing."[17] Using the Lean Startup techniques outlined in Chapter 4, these nimble, interdisciplinary teams worked in a highly iterative fashion with very short-term deadlines.[18] Soon several HHS data sets were available to the public; the platform was beginning to take shape.

But there was a problem. Although data was being "liberated," few people outside of HHS realized that it was available, and a platform is

---

16. Talk at TechCrunch Disrupt 2012, http://techcrunch.com/2012/05/23/us-cto-todd-park-obama-has-a-very-high-geek-quotient-but-its-all-a-means-to-an-end/.

17. Simon Owens, "Can Todd Park Revolutionize the Health Care Industry?" *Atlantic,* June 2011, www.theatlantic.com/technology/archive/2011/06/can-todd-park-revolutionize-the-health-care-industry/239708/.

18. From an interview with Brynn Koeppen, "Todd Park on Entrepreneurship, Mobility and 'Health Datapalooza,'" published in "Execs to Know, Information Tech, Mobility, Small Business," January 4, 2012, www.washingtonexec.com/2012/01/todd-park-on-entrepreneurship-mobility-and-health-datapalooza.

not very useful without applications. So once again, Park had to create customers. Using his extensive government and industry contacts, he put together a meeting of experts in the health care industry and experts in analyzing and using Big Data—two groups of people who had never met each other before. The group brainstormed about ways to use HHS data and came up with many potential applications. Park issued a challenge to those present: Can you turn your idea into a live application in 90 days?

Three months later, in June 2010, the first "Health Datapalooza" showcased the applications that were being developed. Several were real products that were already working and had viable business models to fund their growth. For example, the first version of iTriage, a popular application that catalogs everything from symptoms to doctors to drugs, was developed in the 90-day period and demonstrated at the event. Todd Park had created customers for HHS's data platform—entrepreneurial companies eager to develop applications—by making available both the data and the publicity they needed to start their new businesses.

The popularity of the data platform enticed more developers within HHS to join "data liberation" teams, and the platform expanded. The second Datapalooza was held in June 2011. Proposals for *TED*-style talks about useful applications using HHS data were solicited, and so many were submitted that an *American Idol*-style selection process was needed to choose the top 50. The virtuous circle started picking up speed. The third Datapalooza in June 2012 lasted two days and attracted 1,600 people. A vibrant ecosystem had developed around the HHS data platform; in the conference keynote, Park proudly declared that progress was "out of control." But by this time, Park was no longer working at HHS; he had recently been asked to work the same magic for the whole federal government. He had become the Chief Technology Officer of the United States.

Think about it. In three years, Todd Park created a self-sustaining platform that would form the basis of many new businesses, while empowering entrepreneurial teams inside of HHS. He was able to bring together different constituencies and turn them into mutual customers because he understood health care, understood data, and understood that the right business for HHS to be in was making its data available on a public platform. Rather than devising plans and generating RFPs, Todd Park sparked imaginations and gave people permission to act.

 Anna: It's difficult to see how HHS had the resources to do all of this. Todd Park didn't seem to do any planning or have much of a budget.

M&T: Park was technically savvy enough to use a platform strategy. Most of the platform was already in place—the part that gathered and aggregated the data. The entrepreneurial teams he recruited simply exposed data sets through a Web site. This is something that small teams can do quickly without a lot of money. The HHS teams worked directly with the businesses creating applications that used their data to find out what data was needed, in what format, how often, and so on. This rapid feedback from people who used their data energized the HHS teams, and energized people can accomplish a lot of work.

Otto: Did the HHS teams stay energized after Todd Park left?

M&T: All the evidence says that the HHS health data initiative is alive and well and growing faster than ever. There's a reason for this. Peter Drucker said that once business leaders decide what business they are in, the next step is to put work systems in place that allow people to convert the new strategy from an idea into an ongoing business.[19] Todd Park created effective, cooperative work systems that were supported and expanded after he left.

The Rise of Rational Work Systems

The rise of rational economics in the 1970s did more than enshrine the principle of maximizing shareholder value in corporate governance systems. Rational economics cascaded down through the work systems of corporations as well. It all started with the idea that rational people are utility maximizers—they make decisions that favor their personal best interests. It's a small step to conclude that utility maximizers are probably shirkers—people who try to get as much economic benefit as they can in exchange for as little work as they can get away with.

According to Dale Miller of Princeton University,[20] "The ideology of self-interest, widely celebrated in individualistic cultures, functions as a powerful self-fulfilling force." In other words, the assumption that people are inherently selfish has been so widely repeated that it has come to be accepted as fact. As a consequence, starting in the 1970s

---

19. Drucker, *Management*.
20. See Dale T. Miller, "The Norm of Self-Interest," *American Psychologist*, December 1999.

and 1980s, work systems increasingly came under the influence of rational models, especially in Western businesses.

How do rational work systems operate? If a company believes that front-line workers will do their best to get as much as they can and in return do as little work as they can get away with, it has two options: Either the company can provide workers with detailed direction and close supervision, or else it can devise an incentive system to align the best interests of the workers with the best interests of the company.

Companies that choose the first option design scripted work practices that have little tolerance for variation. Since independent decisions are assumed to be biased toward the best interests of the decision maker, workers are discouraged from making changes to their work practices, and their work is usually measured against a standard. These kinds of work practices telegraph the message that workers are not supposed to think for themselves, so the companies that use them have a difficult time tapping into the intelligence and ingenuity of their workforce.

Self-Fulfilling Prophecies

 A second option for a company concerned about shirking is to set up an incentive system focused on individual performance. The problem with this option is that it sends workers a clear message: *We don't believe you will give your best effort voluntarily—in fact, we expect you to hold back and avoid doing anything unless it increases your incentive pay.* Workers hear this message loud and clear, and it doesn't take long for the presumption of shirking to become a self-fulfilling prophecy. To make things worse, a system that pays individuals for performance attracts the portion of the population that will not perform well unless they are paid extra to do so. So incentive pay actually *attracts* shirkers—a second self-fulfilling prophecy.

Research has shown that extrinsic motivation (rewards) rapidly "crowds out" intrinsic motivation (enjoyment).[21] So if you introduce incentives to a group of energized workers, the energy is likely to dissipate and collaboration is sure to die. And once extinguished, the spark of enthusiasm that workers got from pride in doing a good job is very hard to reignite.

---

21. B. S. Frey and R. Jegen, "Motivation Crowding Theory," *Journal of Economic Surveys* 15, no. 5 (2001): 589–611.

After a while, most workers see incentives as a game, and too often they are better at playing the game than their managers are at devising it. Gaming the system becomes a common practice—and self-interest becomes a self-fulfilling prophecy.

There is yet another problem with incentive systems: It is incredibly difficult to make them fair. If an incentive system is not considered "fair," it will trigger a strong backlash from those who believe that their contributions are "unfairly" treated, and those contributions will not be forthcoming in the future. Thus, it should be no surprise that incentives tend to decrease performance in environments that require collaboration.

Research has shown that the presumption of selfishness is true for maybe 30% of most populations; another 50% are reliably unselfish, and the remaining 20% could go either way, depending on the context.[22] If a company presumes that the undecided 20% are selfish, you can bet they will be selfish—it's a self-fulfilling prophecy. But worse, the company will create an environment where the 50% of the people who are unselfish are forced to act selfishly. And losing the energy, commitment, and intelligence of half the workforce is perhaps the biggest and most tragic self-fulfilling prophecy of them all.

Anna: I heard you say that 30% of my workforce could be selfish. Don't I need to make sure I get the most out of those workers?

M&T: Just as the assumption of selfish behavior is a self-fulfilling prophecy, the assumption that people are eager to do good work is also a self-fulfilling prophecy. If you assume the best in your workforce and create a climate where people are trusted to do their best work, you will find most people are eager to do a good job. Those few who are inclined to do as little as possible will feel pressure from their peers to do their fair share. They are likely to comply, or they may look for jobs in other companies. Either way, you won't have very many shirkers.

Otto: So if rational work systems don't work well, what does?

M&T: Reciprocity—the idea that people who are well treated respond in kind. Companies that treat their employees well find that those employees treat the company—and its customers—well in return. In the long run, reciprocity tends to work much better than incentives.

---

22. Yochai Benkler, "The Unselfish Gene," *Harvard Business Review*, July–August 2011.

Not All Profits Are Created Equal

In his book *The Ultimate Question 2.0* Fred Reichheld writes that there are two kinds of profits: good profits and bad profits.[23] Good profits come from delighted customers who feel they have received fair value for their money. Bad profits come from customers who are annoyed by things such as nuisance fees, onerous contracts, and poor service. While many companies might look at all profits as being the same, Reichheld notes that bad profits decrease customer loyalty and result in negative recommendations, and they demoralize employees as well. In industries where customers have a choice, bad profits generally result in lower profitability.

Michael Raynor and Mumtaz Ahmed of Deloitte found approximately the same thing. They studied the performance of more than 25,000 companies from 1966 to 2010, looking for common strategies of companies that were truly successful over the long term. In the end, they could find only two:[24]

- Better before cheaper—compete on value rather than price.
- Revenue before cost—prioritize increasing revenue over reducing cost.

In other words, profits that come from delivering more products that customers value are better than profits that come from cutting costs.

Zeynep Ton of the MIT Sloan School of Management agrees. He compared retail stores in the United States and Europe and reports that the stores that invest in their employees do far better than those that focus on cutting labor costs.[25] In one example, a retail chain that pays 40% higher salaries than competitors has two-thirds higher sales per square foot. Another chain that pays employees twice as much as competitors has three times the sales per square foot of those competitors. A large retailer found that a $1 increase in payroll was likely to generate between $4 and $28 in increased sales.

How can higher labor costs result in higher profits? It's a virtuous circle: High labor budgets result in good quality and quantity of labor, which result in good operational execution, which results in high

---

23. Fred Reichheld, *The Ultimate Question 2.0* (Harvard Business Review Press, 2011).
24. Michael Raynor and Mumtaz Ahmed, "Three Rules for Making a Company Truly Great," *Harvard Business Review*, April 2013.
25. Zeynep Ton, "Why 'Good Jobs' Are Good for Retailers," *Harvard Business Review*, January–February 2013.

sales and profits.[26] Ton's exemplary retail chains provide full-time jobs with benefits, reliable scheduling, higher staffing levels, and much more training. These factors make it possible for employees to keep the shelves stocked and help customers when they need it. Employees are often buyers for their departments and can fill in at many different jobs. They are expected to act on customer feedback and help improve their processes. Overall, valued employees and effective work practices combine to create stores where customers find what they want and are pleased with the experience. It all adds up to sustainable profits.

> **Anna:** Those things might work for stores and restaurants, but what about design and development? How do you get the best results there?
>
> **M&T:** Product development is always a team effort; in fact, it usually involves multiple teams from different disciplines. So the best work systems for development are ones that promote communication and cooperation.

Case: Working Together at Ford

Alan Mulally spent most of his career at Boeing. He was the Chief Engineer and Program Manager of the hugely successful Boeing 777 development program in the early 1990s and went on to head up the Commercial Aviation Division. Mulally had attended the Sloan Fellows Program at the MIT Sloan School of Management in 1982, and for a thesis, he studied Southwest Airlines—in particular, its charismatic leader, Herb Kelleher.

Southwest Airlines is an excellent example of a reliably profitable business in a reliably unprofitable industry. Known in the airline industry for its superb operations, Southwest is more widely known by customers for its energized, fun-loving employees. This is the business model that Mulally decided to use. Throughout his career he emphasized group cohesiveness rather than individual incentives; his signature initiative at Boeing was called "Working Together."[27]

Looking back, it's easy to wonder why Mulally wasn't chosen as CEO of Boeing in 2005, but events conspired to encourage the board

---

26. Ibid.
27. Mary and Tom Poppendieck, *Leading Lean Software Development* (Addison-Wesley, 2010), Chapter 1.

to select an outsider. Some 3,000 miles away in Detroit, Bill Ford Jr. was looking for someone to take over his job as CEO of Ford. The company was sinking deeper and deeper into trouble, and Ford was unable to turn it around, so he convinced Mulally to give it a try.[28] Ford told Mulally that his biggest problems would be corporate silos, executives posturing for personal advantage, and a culture of hiding problems. If ever there was a work system built on the rational model, this was it.

 Mulally set out to change Ford's culture to one of interdisciplinary teamwork that encouraged exposing problems and working together to solve them. His message was that there is only "One Ford." He immediately started holding short, mandatory weekly meetings with his executive team. Each meeting was focused on exposing problems and finding solutions, and every executive at the meeting was expected to be personally knowledgeable about the details of his or her area of responsibility and prepared to make decisions. At the first meeting, Mulally posted a set of ten rules:

1. People first
2. Everyone is included
3. Compelling vision
4. Clear performance goals
5. One plan
6. Facts and data
7. Propose a plan; "find a way" attitude
8. Respect, listen, help, and appreciate each other
9. Emotional resilience . . . trust the process
10. Have fun . . . enjoy the journey and each other

Over time Mulally restructured the executive team to include a matrix of geographic areas and skill areas (e.g., product development, manufacturing, and marketing). Executives found that in order to be prepared for their weekly meetings, they had to have similar meetings, reflecting a corresponding interdisciplinary structure and problem-solving approach. As time went on, both the matrix structure and the

---

28. Information in this section is from Bryce G. Hoffman, *American Icon: Alan Mulally and the Fight to Save Ford Motor Company* (Crown Business, 2012).

focused meetings cascaded downward throughout the company, encouraging cross-disciplinary problem solving at every level.

The cultural change that Mulally brought to Ford spread through the company in a remarkably short time, and the results are history: Mulally led one of the most successful corporate turnarounds in U.S. history, avoiding disaster during the financial crisis of 2008 and emerging to field a simplified yet very strong lineup of vehicles that people love.

Otto: Did average workers really see the cultural change at Ford?

M&T: Definitely. When we attended a conference at the Ford Auditorium four years after Mulally joined Ford, we heard the same story from several people: "Alan Mulally has made this company a great place to work. Finally, I love coming to work in the morning."

Anna: How was it possible for one person to change the culture at a company that fast—even a CEO? Did Mulally bring in a new team?

M&T: Actually, Mulally kept the existing executive team largely intact at first; it changed gradually over time. What he did was change the expectations; Mulally created an environment where people were expected to cooperate with each other. Instead of focusing on individual metrics, executives were expected to be frank about their problems and cooperate with each other to solve these problems on a week-to-week basis. Since cooperative behavior was constantly being modeled at the top of the company, a strong signal was sent to the organization that "working together" was the expected behavior at all levels.

Otto: So it sounds like teamwork is important at Ford.

M&T: Alan Mulally believes that skilled and motivated teams are the key to Ford's future.[29] Teamwork is important in any complex environment, because if you optimize any individual area of a complex system, you will necessarily suboptimize the whole system. Whenever complexity or collaboration is involved, work systems that focus on cooperation and teamwork are much more effective than those that focus on individual performance.

---

29. From the Ford Web site. See http://corporate.ford.com/careers/careers-news-detail/careers-alan-mulally-videos?&ccode=US.

Cooperative Work Systems

Economists like to study **social dilemmas,** problems that arise when the interests of individuals are at odds with the interests of a larger group. The classic economic theory on social dilemmas is called the **tragedy of the commons.** This theory holds that commons—areas that are the joint responsibility of a community—are not sustainable without management oversight. Why not? When individuals have no incentive to limit their use of common areas to their fair share, or to contribute their fair share to the upkeep of the common areas, the commons will deteriorate over time through some combination of abuse, neglect, and overuse. Or so the theory goes.

Governing the Commons

 Elinor Ostrom didn't believe that the tragedy of the commons was necessarily true in real life, so she set out to find counterexamples. She won the Nobel Prize in Economics in 2009 for her lifelong work of studying local governance mechanisms aimed at preserving shared resources. She studied communities that have successfully maintained common areas—fishing waters, forests, grazing lands, irrigation systems—for decades or even centuries. She concluded that local groups are much more effective at regulating common areas than a central bureaucracy.

Ostrom summarized her findings in a list of eight principles that successful self-governing communities have in common:[30]

1. There are clearly defined community boundaries.
2. There are rules of use that are well matched to the local conditions.
3. Most individuals affected by these rules can participate in modifying the rules.
4. Community members set up a system for monitoring compliance.
5. A system of graduated sanctions is used.
6. Low-cost conflict resolution mechanisms are available.

---

30. Elinor Ostrom, *Governing the Commons: The Evolution of Institutions for Collective Action* (Cambridge University Press, 1990).

7. External authorities respect the right of the community to devise its own rules.

8. Governance activities are organized in multiple layers of nested enterprises.

> **Anna:** Do these communities maintain common properties without any controls? No rules? Or if there are rules, no one to enforce them?
>
> **M&T:** In the areas Ostrom studied, there were rules and there was enforcement to be sure that the rules were followed. But the rules were decided upon and enforced by the local community of users, not an external authority or a bureaucracy. Think of it as governance through peer pressure.

Peer Pressure

Until recently, most of the research in economics treated groups as collections of individuals—there was little thought given to the concept that a group can have behavioral characteristics of its own, and this behavior might be independent of the individuals in the group. But Robert Sampson of Harvard University had a hunch that neighborhoods might have a set of characteristics that are independent of the people living there. So he led a comprehensive study on cooperative behavior in the neighborhoods in Chicago starting in 1995.

Sampson measured a characteristic of neighborhoods that he calls **collective efficacy**, a combination of two mechanisms: **social cohesion** and **shared expectations for control**.[31] So what is collective efficacy? It is the extent to which cohesive groups control bad behavior through self-enforcing group norms and expectations; or, to put it more simply, it is the judicious use of **peer pressure** by a like-minded group of people. Sampson found that some Chicago neighborhoods have high collective efficacy and some have much lower collective efficacy; further, he found that high collective efficacy is a key contributor to community well-being. In other words, communities that control bad behavior through peer pressure are better off than communities where people expect outsiders to make and enforce the rules.

---

31. Robert J. Sampson, *Great American City: Chicago and the Enduring Neighborhood Effect* (The University of Chicago Press, 2012).

It doesn't seem like much of a leap to think of companies as neighborhoods and to consider the collective efficacy of an organization. To see how a company with high collective efficacy might operate, let's consider a well-known example: W. L. Gore & Associates. This $2.5 billion chemical products company has never failed to make a profit in its 65 years of existence—yet it operates without a management hierarchy. At Gore:

- People choose their own work.
- Leaders are those who attract followers.
- Individual business units are small, self-governing, and self-supporting.

How can this possibly work? At Gore, the prosperity of individual workers is determined by the economic success of their small (less than 150 people) business unit. Because of this, people in every department—from engineering to manufacturing to sales—work together to ensure the success of their business unit. People at the company have come to believe that "peer pressure is much more effective than a concept of a boss. Many, many times more powerful."[32]

A peer culture is not unique to Gore. It can be found at many startup companies. It is common in university research communities. It is the hallmark of most open source projects. The work systems at Gore might be thought of as an anomaly in the business world, but they are relatively common in small businesses, nonprofits, academic institutions, and even local governments of small communities.

Just because an organization lacks a hierarchical governance structure does not mean there is no governance. Strong norms of behavior designed and monitored by people with mutual interests work just as well, maybe even better.[33] In fact, this is exactly the way Sampson's research shows that collective efficacy works.

 Otto: Is peer pressure the reason for Alan Mulally's weekly meetings? Would copying those weekly meetings be a good start?

---

32. Malcolm Gladwell, *Tipping Point: How Little Things Can Make a Big Difference* (Little, Brown and Company, 2002), p. 186.
33. Of course, strong group norms can also suppress individual ideas and motivation. Replacing hierarchical governance with peer pressure is not a panacea for solving all problems.

M&T: With all due respect to Alan Mulally, we don't recommend blindly copying his practices. With decades of experience, he knew instinctively how to proceed, but you can be sure that there are more nuisances in those weekly meetings than meet the eye. It is not a good idea to copy specific practices; it is much safer to uncover the thinking behind successful approaches and mindfully apply that thinking to your problems.

For example, before you copy Gore's maximum group size, be sure to understand the thinking behind the company's practice of splitting its business units when they reach approximately 150 people.

The Dunbar Number

Early in his career, Robin Dunbar, a British anthropologist, found himself observing the social dynamics of gelada baboons in Ethiopia, hoping his work might shed light on the evolution of humans. Over time, Dunbar noticed that different species of monkeys, baboons, and apes tended to live in different-size groups (or troops). Interestingly, the size of a troop seemed to be related to the size of the species' brain, or more specifically, the size of the neocortex, the outer part of the brain that controls thought and language. Primates that lived in larger troops also tended to have a larger neocortex.

Dunbar theorized that primate brains evolved to be quite large so that individuals could keep track of their social relationships with others in their troop. The obvious next step, with humans at the top of the primate evolutionary chain, was to project the community size that humans might gravitate toward, based on the relative size of the human neocortex. The answer that popped out of Dunbar's calculations was . . . 150, which is now called the Dunbar Number.

Dunbar proposed a theory: The human mind evolved to be capable of tracking the social relationships among approximately 150 people. To check out this theory, he and other researchers started looking at the size of social groups of people in preindustrial societies, especially hunter-gatherers. They found several common sizes:

1. An "inner circle" of about three to five very close friends or family members
2. A "sympathy group" of 12 to 15 close friends who care about each other's fate

3. A "hunting group" of 30 to 50 colleagues who cooperate to accomplish a task

4. A "clan" of 150 people who maintain stable interpersonal relationships

5. A "tribe" of about 500 to 2,500 people who speak the same language or dialect

Voilà! Dunbar's Number appeared to be the size of a "clan," a group of people who know each other well, help each other out, and share important ceremonies.

Reciprocity

 So what does brain size have to do with community size? The theory goes something like this: **Reciprocity is the currency of cooperation.** At the simplest level, this means that if I do you a favor, you are expected to return the favor in the future. But reciprocity can get more complex. Let's say that I do a good deed for someone close to you, and later on, you do something good for me to return the favor. Or perhaps I cooperate in a group activity such as hunting, expecting to benefit from a successful hunt. These more complicated exchanges are forms of indirect (or generalized) reciprocity, and this more nuanced reciprocity works only when people can keep tabs on who can be trusted and who owes what to whom.

Dunbar believes that the size of the neocortex in a monkey or baboon or person determines the number of social relationships it can track at one time, and hence the size of the group within which generalized reciprocity will work. Humans can track the social relationships of about 150 people; when you get more than 150, you start to need authority and policing to enforce good behavior. But below 150, everybody knows everyone else, and social relationships are adequate to keep the reciprocity tally in balance.

There is contemporary evidence that this is true. The Hutterites, a religious group that forms self-sufficient agricultural communities in Europe and North America, have kept their communities under 150 people for centuries. Beyond religious communities, Dunbar found that during the eighteenth century, the average number of people in villages in every English county except Kent was around 160. (In Kent it was 100.) Even today, army companies average around 150 and academic communities that are focused on a particular narrow discipline tend to be between 100 and 200; when the community gets larger, it tends to split into subdisciplines.[34]

> **Anna:** Is reciprocity really practical in the business world? **M&T:** There's a lot more reciprocity used in business than you might think. Most salespeople know that if they take care of their customers, the customers will be more likely to order from them. Good team leaders know that if they take care of their teams, the team members are likely to come through for them. And companies that take good care of their employees find that the employees have an increased interest in helping the company be successful.

The Rules of Cooperation

Robin Dunbar's research on group size and reciprocity, Elinor Ostrom's research on how communities maintain common resources, and Robert Sampson's work on neighborhoods are foundational works in the science of cooperation. All three are based on extensive studies of communities in the field rather than extrapolations from observations of individuals in contrived situations. Let's summarize their findings:

1. A work group or community should be responsible for its own fate—insofar as this is practical. For example, a product team should include all functions necessary to design, develop, deliver, and maintain the product. We have found that the hunting group size (30 to 50) is a good size for a product team.

2. Rules and norms should be well matched to local conditions; they should be determined, or at least adapted, by the people they affect. This implies that teams should design and adapt their own processes to match their particular circumstances.

3. There should be an expectation that rules will be followed and that peers will monitor each other's behavior. We have found that peer pressure occurs naturally when team members believe the rules are appropriate (because they helped craft them) and they care about the success of their work.

---

34. See Robin Dunbar, *How Many Friends Does One Person Need?* (Harvard University Press, 2010).

4. External authorities should respect the right of the community to devise its own rules. The idea that there should be standard processes across a company is not compatible with this model of local responsibility; instead, local groups are trusted to devise work practices best suited to their situation.

 Otto: You know, that sounds like the way things get done in the groups I hang out with outside of work. M&T: Exactly. A good place to see how cooperation actually works is to watch it in action when participation in an activity is optional. When people volunteer their time, leadership practices that foster cooperation are the only ones that work. Businesses can learn a lot about organizing work teams from successful volunteer organizations. Peter Drucker once suggested that managers should treat knowledge workers as if they were volunteers, because in fact they are volunteers.

Case: When Workers Are Volunteers

Joe Justice knows a lot about treating people like volunteers—he heads up an army of them. An agile consultant by day, on nights and weekends Joe spends his time trying to make a dent in the environmental impact of automobiles. He plans to do this with a car called WIKISPEED, a modular vehicle designed to be built in a garage with inexpensive tools and materials, and to travel over 100 miles on a gallon of gas (that's 2⅓ liters per 100 kilometers).

Joe discovered that the agile techniques he uses when working with software teams are just the thing for organizing the WIKISPEED crew of a couple of hundred volunteers spread around the world. He found that Scrum—a set of agile practices—gives him a way to establish distributed collaborative teams very quickly and with little overhead, because it provides the minimum set of tools to help team members work well together. He uses Kanban—an agile scheduling technique—to optimize the flow of work within a team. He discovered that principles from Extreme Programming (XP)—especially test-first development—inspire technical practices that create top-quality work. And using principles from lean, WIKISPEED teams are able to maximize the amount of time spent creatively solving problems.

Joe Justice did not learn about agile methods in his computer science curriculum in college, but when he started his career, he got a job at an agile company. "I didn't know what agile was; it was just the way work was done," he said. "Later, when I was coordinating deliveries with other teams, I was surprised to see how often they were working late or even working weekends. The teams I was on were going home at five and the clients loved us! I started reading about project management to understand what was so different, and I realized those teams were beholden to a waterfall schedule agreed to years in advance while my teams had permission to iterate and plan incrementally."

Joe Justice's first big project was writing the titling registration system for the state of Colorado; his job was to encode in software the regulations for road-legal vehicles. He liked this job because he loved cars; he enjoyed rebuilding cars to improve their performance. About this time, Joe heard about the Progressive Insurance Automotive X PRIZE—a challenge with a purse of $10 million designed to encourage the development of highly efficient, commercially viable, road-legal cars. All that knowledge from his day job, combined with his love of cars, added up to a simple conclusion: Joe knew he had to take up the challenge. He sent in his application and began building a car in his garage.

Computer-savvy guy that he was, Joe posted his progress on a blog, and to his delight, he started getting help. Soon over 40 people from around the world were commenting on his designs and helping to build parts. You would think that a distributed team building a car would be an unlikely crew, but Joe knew a thing or two about distributed teams. He was familiar with the kind of systems architecture that works well in a distributed environment, and he had plenty of evidence that the best way to solve complex problems is through rapid iteration. Finally, he knew the advantages of minimizing the cost of change. Therefore, he designed the car around modular subsystems with standard interfaces so that individual modules could be hot-swapped quickly and easily. "We can change suspension systems in about the time it takes to change a tire," Joe Justice claims. And at the X PRIZE grounds, he had the opportunity to prove his claim.

In early May 2010, 16 members of the WIKISPEED team showed up for the X PRIZE competition at the Michigan International Speedway, many of them meeting each other in person for the first time. When the car needed modifications, the team swarmed the problem and rebuilt the car in 48 hours, which made a deep impression on automotive experts at the site. The WIKISPEED car did not win the competition, but it got a huge amount of publicity and many more volunteers. The team turned its focus on the real goal: Make a difference in the environment by developing a fuel-efficient car that can be built by ordinary people and modified easily, one module at a time.

Team WIKISPEED has made steady progress ever since. The boxy exterior gave way to a sporty shell for the Detroit auto show; a classy family sedan and a commercial truck are on the way. Each module has undergone several revisions, and development sites have been added or expanded. An agreement with Open Source Ecology means that most WIKISPEED plans are publicly available—making it possible for anyone to build his or her own car.

Anna: Why do people volunteer to work on WIKISPEED?
Joe: We try to do something worth doing, and that seems to allow people the opportunity to opt in and turn loose the interest they already have. And maybe that's the biggest shock—that there are so many people out there who can't wait to do something like this, who are beating down the door. . . . The peak of Maslow's Hierarchy of Needs is self-actualization, and a lot of folks don't feel that when their company's mission statement is "Make more dollars for shareholders."

Otto: How do you keep volunteers engaged?
Joe: Morale is a multiplier of velocity, so it's worth paying attention to. The agile toolkit that the community has built up over the years aids morale and aids high-morale teams. Demonstrating regular successes is one piece that agile does very well. At regular demos, team members are encouraged to invite their stakeholders or their customers. The entire team gets to be present, and often the people who did the work get to do the demo. That seems to keep this sense of ownership alive.

The visibility from frequent standup meetings (in our case they're weekly) lets people feel associated with the entire project. Pairing helps build mutual team respect, and then rotating pairs helps propagate that and it also builds cross-functional teams. What I believe keeps a lot of people around are the pieces in the agile toolkit that keep morale high and that help people feel themselves becoming more skillful as they get to go deeper and become more cross-functional. Getting to celebrate their successes is also part of the process.

Anna: How do you coordinate a distributed hardware team?
Joe: For hardware projects, we first split the hardware problem into modules. Each area that is likely to change is logically split into its own module and packaged with the stuff

that would also change at the same time. For example, the engine module of the WIKISPEED car contains the engine, fuel system, and cooling system; all three systems would likely change together if we switched from gasoline to electric or biodiesel. We avoid Big Design Up Front, but we do practice contract-first development, designing the interfaces between modules before anything else. Then we start rapidly iterating each module with emergent architecture inside each module. This is the way modern software teams work, especially for Web-service-based solutions.

 Otto: What kind of communication tools do you use?

Joe: Every aspect of WIKISPEED is built to reduce the level of effort required to join or leave the team and to blur the line between anyone out there in the world and an active team member. Everybody connects with everybody depending on the communication tools that they love to use. Everybody has access to a team Google group, so there's a lively thread of e-mail discussions. Then there are updates on Facebook and on YouTube and on Twitter. We intentionally try to build a virtual room where everyone is in earshot and eyesight of everyone else at all times, so there's chatter flowing past that has nothing to do with the task that most people are on, but they are aware of it. So they have this concept of this larger distributed project—that's motivating all by itself. A team room is a wonderful velocity and morale builder, and we try to approximate that through online tools. There are many free tools that do it pretty well.

Anna: Why are you making WIKISPEED plans publicly available?

Joe: If we aren't public about our developments, we'd lose the ability for people around the world to most rapidly engage. When we make something new available, we have all these people out in the world who are able to look at that and say, "That's neat, I want to get involved in that." And they're able to because it's as transparent as possible. If we made our project less transparent, our velocity will suffer. And one of our superpowers is that we're able to develop really fast. Why would we compromise that?

Every time we innovate something we say, "Is this something that a sophisticated manufacturer could understand in less than a month?" The answer is almost always yes. Then we say to ourselves, "What's the value of hiding it?" Competing companies would then simply reverse-engineer our solution. We'd rather they spend that time building on a solution and innovating.

Otto: What are your key learnings from WIKISPEED?
Joe: I learned to split problems into small modules that small teams can work on and focus on designing interfaces between teams first. And I learned a lot about leadership. I learned that a leader should

- Do something that's worth doing
- Unleash the interest that people already have
- Increase morale—because it is a multiplier of velocity
- Demonstrate and publicize regular success
- Solve complex problems with rapid iteration
- Minimize the cost of change
- Simulate colocation
- Provide transparency because it invites engagement
- Let people see they are part of a larger whole

Questions to Ponder

1. What business are you in? What is the purpose of your organization? Does this purpose inspire you to come to work in the morning? Does it inspire others?

2. How well do "ordinary" workers in your organization understand how their work helps achieve the organization's purpose? Do they understand what their ultimate customers will value? Do they see the impact of their work—the value it delivers?

3. What is it that keeps people engaged and contributing their best efforts toward the success of your organization? Do you attempt to do this through an individual incentive bonus system? If so, how is it working for you?

4. What does the word *team* mean in your company? How large are your teams?

5. How loosely coupled are your teams? How loosely coupled is your system architecture? Does your team architecture match your system architecture? (This is called Conway's Law.)

6. Do you have "product" teams that can design, develop, and deliver a product or service or specific customer value to the market? How well are they working?

CHAPTER 1 THE PURPOSE OF BUSINESS **37**

7. What does the term *self-organizing team* mean to you? Do you have such teams? How well are they working? What might make them work better?

8. Do your teams have rules that team members are expected to follow? Where do they come from? Are they contentious? Are they enforced? Are they working?

9. Do people regard your company as a great place to work? How do you know?

10. Imagine that everyone in your group won the lottery next week. Would they continue to come to work? What would make your workplace so attractive that people would be eager to show up, to put in their best efforts, to stay late—even after they win the lottery?

2

Energized Workers

Full Potential

In 1989 students from Garfield High School took more than 450 Advanced Placement (AP) tests in 16 different subjects to gain college credit for their high school work. Eleven years earlier, Garfield students had taken a grand total of 10 AP tests. Clearly a dramatic change had occurred at the school during the 1980s. It wasn't the school's building or the size of its budget. It certainly wasn't the neighborhood, a poor Hispanic barrio on the east side of Los Angeles. According to people who were there at the time, the dramatic change at Garfield High School can be attributed to *ganas.*

 Ganas is a Spanish word that captures the mindset of people who are determined to reach a goal and willing to work hard to achieve it. At Garfield High School in the 1980s, a handful of teachers and administrators believed that the best way to help students reach their full potential was to develop *ganas* in each student. Rather than focusing on students identified as "gifted and talented," they created challenging courses that catered to any student who was eager for a better future and willing to work hard to get there.

The story begins some years earlier, when Henry Gradillas was a teenager growing up in a similarly poor Hispanic neighborhood. One of his first trips out of the barrio was to do some painting for his tenth-grade life sciences teacher. Gradillas was amazed at the size of his teacher's house and its furnishings. He asked his teacher, "How can your family have a lifestyle so much better than mine?" The answer was: education. Both the teacher and his wife had college degrees that led to well-paying jobs. So Gradillas decided he would get a college degree. He was surprised to learn that he had been "tracked" into the least demanding classes the school system had to offer—someone had decided that he didn't have the talent to take demanding classes. Gradillas had to fight to get into college preparatory classes and take remedial courses to catch up. But he got that college degree and found it was indeed a ticket to a much better life.

When Gradillas became principal at Garfield High School in 1981, he believed it was his job to give every one of the kids in the school the same chance he had at their age. He created a disciplined environment by stopping drug dealing and gang activity as well as tardiness and absenteeism. He did not allow underperforming students in extracurricular activities and arranged for remedial courses instead. He shut down undemanding science and math classes and required students to pass algebra in order to graduate. He limited time spent in nonacademic classes and required every class to have content that prepared students for well-paying jobs. He encouraged teachers to offer AP classes for students who wanted to earn college credit and gave them time to attract students to these classes.

It was in this environment that a remarkable teacher, Jaime Escalante, flourished. Before Gradillas arrived, Escalante had been struggling to teach AP calculus, one of the most demanding AP subjects, with little or no support from administrators. In fact, he had been warned that his challenging course would break the fragile egos of poor Hispanic students, and he was advised to offer much easier classes. But Escalante had taught mathematics for years in his native Bolivia, and he was not going to offer students in Los Angeles less demanding classes than he taught in La Paz. Where others saw weak students in need of coddling, Escalante saw bright kids—often well educated in their home countries—who were eager for a challenge.

Escalante thought of himself as a coach and treated his students as a team training for the challenge of taking the AP calculus exam each May. Just to get onto the calculus team, students had to take two full years of algebra and master geometry and trigonometry during intense summer sessions. Calculus students—and their parents—signed a contract agreeing to do daily homework and attend after-school and Saturday morning study sessions. Why would students work so hard? So they could get accepted into college, earn scholarships, and live a better life. They needed a lot of *ganas* to dedicate so much time to math during their high school years. In 1990 Escalante wrote:

> My sole criterion for acceptance in this program is that the student wants to be a part of it and sincerely wants to learn math. I tell my students, "The only thing you need to have for my program—and you must bring it every day—is *ganas*." . . . I often chose the rascals and kids who were "discipline problems," as well as those who simply liked math. I found that the "class cut-ups" were often the most intelligent, but were extremely bored by poor teaching and disillusioned by the perceived dead-end that school represented for them. Sometimes they showed themselves to have the most *ganas* when their "learning light" finally switched on.[1]

Escalante's math classes grew gradually during his early days at Garfield, but the arrival of Gradillas brought a more disciplined school environment and unconditional support for the challenging math program. In the 1981–82 school year, Escalante had 18 students in his calculus class. In May, all 18 students passed the AP calculus exam, an astounding number for any but the wealthiest high schools in the country. Then, as documented in the movie *Stand and Deliver*, 14 of those students were accused of cheating and their passing grades were withdrawn. Twelve students retook the exam and all of them passed again, with five earning top scores.

The reputation of these students spread and math classes became increasingly popular. In 1987, 129 Garfield students took the AP calculus exam, a number exceeded by only four other schools in the country. Garfield accounted for over 25% of all Hispanics in the country who passed the AP calculus test that year. Meanwhile, other AP classes flourished. Against all odds, Garfield High School sent an astonishingly large percentage of its graduates on to college and distinguished careers.

This story has an epilogue. Gradillas left Garfield in 1987, and support for the math program weakened. Three years later, Escalante also left in frustration, followed a year later by other key teachers in the math program. Although the math program at Garfield suffered, student achievement at the school remained high in the decades that

---

1. Jaime Escalante and Jack Dirmann, "The Jaime Escalante Math Program," *Journal of Negro Education* 59, no. 3 (Summer 1990): 407–23.

followed. Other schools in poor areas throughout the country have cop-
ied the ideas of Gradillas and Escalante, offering challenging classes for
students with the *ganas* to strive to reach their full potential.

 Anna: It sounds to me like the school had a pretty lousy
system for recognizing talented students.

M&T: If talent is something that you discover, rather than
something that you develop, this would be true. But research has shown that talent is not something people are born with;
it is something that is developed over time with hard work and
diligent practice. Unfortunately, many schools create self-fulfilling
prophecies by grouping children according to their perceived potential. Once students are "tracked" as low-potential, they will not be
assigned challenging classes, as Gradillas discovered. Tracking can
start very early and be based on little more than a student's command of English.

Otto: So where does IQ fit into this?

M&T: Good question. IQ scores can also be a self-
fulfilling prophecy. Carol Dweck—whose work we will
look at next—showed that when junior high students
believe their intelligence cannot be changed, it doesn't change.
When they believe—or are taught—that intelligence can be improved
through hard work, their math scores rise.[2]

Ganas *and the Growth Mindset*

You might be wondering what Garfield High School in the 1980s has to
do with business some decades later. To answer this question, consider a
young child who wants to play the piano because she has heard someone else play it beautifully. She sits down at the keyboard and hits the
keys—and it doesn't sound very good. What happens next will determine
whether or not she learns to play the piano. Either she thinks, "I'm no
good at this; I'll go find something else to do that I am good at." Or she
gets the message that no one starts out as a great musician; everyone
has to practice for a long time to become as good as the person who
inspired her. If she starts out with this "growth" mindset, she has a good
chance of becoming a musician.

2. Lisa Blackwell, Kali Trzesniewski, and Carol Dweck, "Implicit Theories of Intelligence Predict Achievement across an Adolescent Transition: A Longitudinal Study
and an Intervention," *Child Development* 78, no. 1 (January–February 2007): 246–63.

In her book *Mindset*,[3] Carol Dweck suggests that when people approach a task, they bring one of two mindsets. There are those who expect to be good at whatever they attempt from the outset. When these people run into situations where they start out rather ineptly and have to work hard to improve, they conclude that the activity must be something they aren't good at, so they abandon it quickly. Dweck calls this kind of thinking the **fixed mindset**.[4] Behind the fixed mindset is the unspoken assumption that talent is something that people either have or they don't, and anyone who has to work hard at something clearly doesn't have the talent for it.

 The second mindset is held by those who believe that with hard work, they can become good at whatever they choose. Dweck calls this attitude the **growth mindset**. You might think of it as an eagerness to improve. Dweck initially encountered this mindset as a young researcher, when she conducted an experiment to investigate how people deal with failure. She gave puzzles to children—first an easy one, then puzzles of increasing difficulty. As they struggled with the more challenging puzzles, Dweck probed to understand how the children were coping with difficulty. She reports:

> Confronted with the hard puzzles, one ten-year-old boy pulled up his chair, rubbed his hands together, smacked his lips, and cried out, "I love a challenge!" Another, sweating away on these puzzles, looked up with a pleased expression and said with authority, "You know, I was *hoping* this would be informative."
>
> *What's wrong with them?* I wondered. I always thought you coped with failure or you didn't cope with failure. I never thought anyone *loved* failure. Were these alien children or were they on to something?[5]

Dweck was determined to figure out what was going on with these children, "to understand the kind of mindset that could turn failure into a gift."

Decades of research by Anders Ericsson, Carol Dweck, and many others have discredited the myth that talent is fixed. Natural talent might help people sail easily through the early stages of learning math or music or martial arts. But inevitably the work gets hard, and at this

3. Carol Dweck, *Mindset: The New Psychology of Success* (Random House, 2006).
4. Ibid.
5. Ibid., Chapter 1.

point those with the fixed mindset are likely to stop trying, while those with a growth mindset work with increasing diligence and keep on improving.

Students in the math program at Garfield developed a growth mindset. They saw that talent was not fixed, that it could be developed through challenging subjects and relentless practice. Everyone in the school saw clearly that learning math was largely a matter of "*ganas:* the desire to learn, the ability to sacrifice, and the wish to get ahead."[6] The students at Garfield who learned to work hard were well equipped to deal with the demands of college courses. In the end, a large portion of Garfield's calculus students moved on to highly successful careers in challenging technical areas.

> Otto: How is a growth mindset related to a lean mindset?
>
> M&T: A company with a lean mindset does not waste time trying to sort out who has more or less talent. It has hiring policies that seek people with *ganas*. It has systems in place that challenge everyone to continually get better at what they do. If you take a look at Southwest Airlines, a company that has historically had a lean mindset, you will probably find many teams that call to mind the team spirit found in Escalante's classrooms.

Can Everybody Be Above Average?

"We have 5,000 workers," someone once told us, "so at least half of them have to be below average." This is an interesting claim, but it is just not true. It is fixed-mindset thinking. Consider Jaime Escalante's math class. If Escalante had compared the students in any class against each other, he would have found that half of them were below the class average. But that's not what he did. He treated each class as a team training to take on the challenge of the AP calculus test in May. He would know how good they were (and how good he was) when the test scores came back. Year in and year out, the entire class scored far above average. He turned a group of kids who were well below average by all objective standards into a group of kids who excelled at the kinds of things that would change their lives:

1. They had developed learning strategies and habits that would last a lifetime.

---

6. Escalante and Dirmann, "The Jaime Escalante Math Program."

2. They were experts in the basic language of science and technology.

3. They had learned to thrive on challenge rather than avoid it.

It is a fixed mindset that compares people against each other and declares that half of them must be below average. At any point in time in any given group, it is true that half of the people *are* below the group average, but that calculation does not take into account their potential. A company with a growth mindset creates an environment in which workers focus on *getting better*, where individuals constantly increase their expertise and teams continuously improve their performance. When the test comes in the marketplace, companies that help all their employees reach their full potential will find that their workforce is far above average.

 Anna: Whenever I do performance appraisals, I'm expected to have an even distribution of results. If I give out more than a couple of "exceeds requirements," the HR people get after me.

M&T: Tell us this: When you hired those people, did you hire an even distribution of people, or did you hire the most talented people you could find?

Anna: The top people, of course.

M&T: So if you hire only top people, how can their talent change so much that within six months to a year, half of those top people have to be below average?

Anna: Good question. I know I have a hard time trying to explain to people during performance reviews that our HR department requires me to fit everyone on a curve. They certainly don't like to hear that.

 Otto: What about a new college graduate who has always been a hard worker? Do companies appreciate people who may not have a lot of experience but are willing to work hard and improve their talent while they are on the job?

M&T: Yes, there are companies like that, and they are good places to work. Let's take a look at a company where the growth mindset was baked into the culture by its founder, starting way back in 1965.

A Challenge That Changed the World

"We've sold area on the silicon wafer for about a billion dollars an acre, that order of magnitude, as long as I've been in the industry,"

Gordon Moore said in 1997.[7] "So if you look at it in a relatively simple-minded manner, you get a pretty good idea of the economics. . . . What really counts is how much stuff we can pack on that area." From these simple economics rose the challenge of Moore's Law: The amount of "stuff" that can be packed into a fixed area of silicon should double every two years, which is the same as saying that the cost of computing should be cut in half every two years.

For four decades, Intel engineers have risen to the challenge, driving the cost of computing relentlessly lower. Moore's Law has provided engineers at Intel with the kind of challenge that keeps a company's innovation machine in high gear. Time and again the limits of Moore's Law have seemed to be approaching, but then a new technology has been invented to keep the momentum going.

Challenges have a way of bringing out the best in people, especially when team members work together to accomplish a deeply meaningful but very difficult goal. As Mihaly Csikszentmihalyi says in his ground-breaking book *Flow*, "The best moments [in our lives] usually occur when a person's body or mind is stretched to its limits in a voluntary effort to accomplish something difficult and worthwhile."[8]

It is not enough to simply provide a challenge; meeting the challenge year after year can happen only in an environment that provides people with the tools and guidance they need to achieve the goal.

Case: Intel's Post-Silicon Validation

Intel's road map calls for a new generation of chips with smaller feature sizes every two years. In 2006 the 65nm generation came out; in 2008 it was the 45nm generation; in 2010 the 32nm generation, in 2012 the 22nm generation, and so on. A major milestone in the development of each new generation is **first silicon**. At this point, the design team can breathe a sigh of relief because finally the product is real—it can be made—and it can be tested. But for the engineers whose job it is to prove that the new product works exactly the way it's supposed to work, first silicon marks the beginning of a period of intense work. Their goal is to qualify the new generation—to reach Product Release

---

7. Intel Developer Conference Keynote, www.intel.com/pressroom/archive/speeches/gem93097.htm.
8. Mihaly Csikszentmihalyi, *Flow: The Psychology of Optimal Experience* (Harper-Collins, 1990).

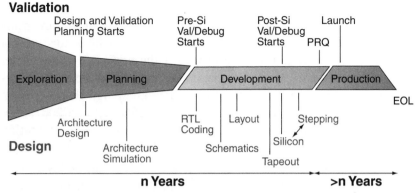

Figure 2-1   Design and validation product life cycle[9]

Qualification (PRQ). Of course, everyone would like this to happen as rapidly as possible so that volume production can begin. (Figure 2-1 depicts the development cycle of one generation.)

The Product Development Engineering (PDE) team in Hillsboro, Oregon, has many dozens of engineers working to qualify new products. They are used to the two-year cycles that are focused on the arrival of first silicon for a new generation and climax during the final drive to qualify the product. The cycle starts when PDE receives enough information about the next-generation product to start preparing for validation, about 18 months before first silicon is scheduled to arrive.

PDE works in a classic embedded software environment—a large amount of software has to be written and tested long before the hardware on which it must run arrives. Not only does the new product have to be tested before it is released to manufacturing, but the system that will test the new product also has to be tested. This is done by placing tens of thousands of the new silicon chips in sockets in system test beds and running the test software to see if the new product is working as expected and if the test system is testing the new product properly. Validation is meticulous, because any defects in the product would be extremely serious. Once the test system is validated, it will be used in manufacturing to run validation tests on the new product generation.

---

9. From J. Keshava, N. Hakim, and C. Prudvi (Intel), "Post-Silicon Validation Challenges: How EDA and Academia Can Help," presented at DAC '10, Anaheim, CA, 2010. Used with permission.

Introducing Agile

It used to be that the Oregon PDE engineers worked nonstop overtime for almost the entire two-year cycle, preparing for silicon for the first 18 months and then getting it to PRQ over the next six months. After two exhausting years, most of the engineers were burned out and interested in jobs with less overtime. PDE leaders knew that they needed a more reliable and sustainable way to develop software, so in 2007, after a grueling two-year cycle, they decided that for the next-generation product they would experiment with agile software development.

Several teams received training in Scrum, which they followed religiously to begin with. After they became familiar with how Scrum worked, they began to adapt it to their unique situation. PDE software engineers liked developing software in two-week increments because it gave them much more control over their work. They could be clear to senior managers about how many features and product variations they could handle, giving executives accurate information about capacity to enable them to make valid trade-off decisions. Both the quantity and quality of the work increased significantly, even while the engineers were working more reasonable hours. The agile experiment was definitely a success.

At the end of the two-year cycle, engineer attrition was lower than normal due to the sustainable pace of the work; this meant that PDE would have more experienced engineers to develop tests for the next-generation product. As the next cycle began, there was time for the agile teams to improve their processes and for agile practices to expand further throughout PDE.

One big change was to form teams that would focus on designing tests for modules or subsystems. Up to that time, the agile teams had been focused on specific functional areas, but that made it difficult to collect all the tests needed by a specific hardware chip or subsystem. Therefore, cross-functional teams were formed to collect functional software (infrastructure and tools) into test modules. Engineers on these teams had a functional home and brought competency from that function to the module team. This significantly improved communication and module integrity.

Second, the teams focused even more effort on integrating and testing software early and often, which had the double benefit of increasing quality *and* reducing the need for testing at the end of development. Throughout the entire two-year cycle, productivity was much higher than in pre-agile days, while PDE teams developed a reputation for delivering virtually defect-free software on time, every time.

Since their software was so reliable, the test engineers began to wonder why it required over a month for manufacturing to validate their code after it was delivered. As they sketched value stream maps with manufacturing to understand what was creating the delay, they discovered that the actual validation time was only three days; most of the time was spent waiting to collect the large number of silicon chips that were needed for validation testing.

As fate would have it, the next product generation was running behind schedule and there was a great desire to shorten its time to manufacturing by several weeks. The PDE manager suggested that a month could be eliminated from the schedule; the only cost would be to make sure that all the silicon needed for validating the test software was available when the software was. This idea was embraced by business managers, and during the last six months of this development cycle, the PDE team was able to reliably move software from development to manufacturing in just a few days—giving the business managers a lot of flexibility.

After two cycles—four years—of hard work, agile development practices were working very well. In fact, the PDE group won a corporate quality award for its outstanding contributions to Intel products.

Next: Triple Productivity

As the next generation of products appeared on the horizon, Moore's Law caught up with PDE. Intel's product design group had gotten very good at creating multiple products from their basic design, so in this generation there would be more products to test. In the previous generation there had been three major products, and each took about three months to validate. So at any given time in the six-month validation period, the PDE group had only two active products to test (see Figure 2-2). The next-generation design would produce eight products, so at any given time during the validation period, six of these could be active—a threefold increase!

Since this workload had to be handled with the same number of people, it required a threefold increase in productivity. Moreover, there would be 20% less laboratory capital, and, of course, customer-measured quality could only increase. The good news was that PDE had 18 months before first silicon arrived to figure out how to triple its productivity during the critical PRQ period.

How do you respond to a challenge like this? PDE created a working group of about 25 engineers—the 3X Working Group—and chartered it

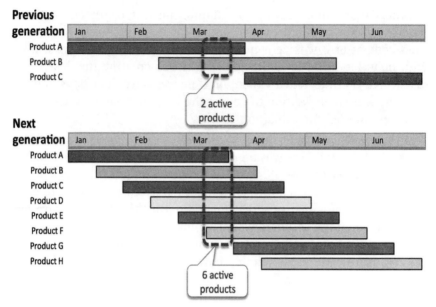

Figure 2-2   Up to three times as many products to test at the same time

to examine PDE work practices and find a way to deliver validated test software at three times the previous pace. The group was coordinated by Patrick Elwer and led by Salman Ahmad, who found the engineers eager to take up the challenge. After all, they would get to revise the work processes they used every day; they were eager to run experiments and find new and better ways of doing their jobs.

The working group leaders knew they needed a disciplined process for reaching the goal, and they had pretty much maximized the benefits they were likely to get out of agile practices. It is common for teams developing embedded software to run up against the limits of agile practices, because they are optimized for software-only products. The PDE group needed an approach that encompassed the entire two-year development cycle and dealt with the fact that the next-generation silicon would not be available for most of that development cycle.

Lean Product Development

PDE chose to use the Lean Product Development techniques recommended by Targeted Convergence Corporation. These techniques consider the entire product—hardware and software—and offer strategies for designing products that take months or years to develop. They focus on continuous improvement of the knowledge used to make decisions, elimination of wishful thinking, and coordination of work across multiple teams. The techniques include LAMDA learning cycles (Look-Ask-Model-Discuss-Act), Knowledge Briefs (a one-page summary of knowledge), Set-Based Design (investigating multiple options to learn as much as possible and decide as late as possible), and Integrating Events (synchronization points where work-to-date is assessed in detail by everyone involved in developing the system and critical decisions are made).[10]

The 3X Working Group started with 16 projects aimed at addressing the most obvious problems. Each project had a Knowledge Brief and a mentor. As the projects got started, it quickly became obvious that increasing productivity by a factor of three might be a great high-level strategy, but it did not provide actionable goals for the projects. Productivity was vague and difficult to measure, and it provided no way for project teams to measure progress or know when they were done.

Ahmad looked carefully at what caused complexity in the environment; he realized that each of the products generated multiple variations that needed testing—for example, different packaging and different die locations required different testing. In the previous generation, there had been 20 of these variations; but in the next generation there would be 64. If the project teams focused on what steps were needed to handle each variation, they would have actionable targets, making it much easier to determine the size of the gaps between present practice and future need, and to track progress in closing the gaps. Ahmad also realized that PDE should assume responsibility for validating each new version of the test software. This meant running over 55,000 silicon chips in a test bed over a weekend—in 48 hours.

With actionable goals in place, the 16 projects were divided into phases:

1. Understand needs.
2. Identify knowledge gaps and propose multiple plans for closing them.
3. Establish at least one feasible approach.
4. Pick the best solution from a system perspective.
5. Get the solution working.

---

10. See Michael Kennedy and Kent Harmon, *Ready, Set, Dominate* (Oaklea Press, 2008). See also www.targetedconvergence.com.

Integrating events, attended by all of the working group teams, were held at the end of each phase. Knowledge of the underlying issues increased rapidly as a result of these events, since many teams discovered that other teams were struggling with the same problems they were. As feasible solutions were proposed, however, it became apparent that many of them had dependencies that reached far outside the working group. Poring through the Knowledge Briefs, Elwer uncovered 20 dependencies and initiated new projects to cover each one.

The biggest dependency turned out to be a key piece of equipment—a robot arm—that would have to reliably place 55,000 silicon units into test sockets during each 48-hour validation period. At the feasibility integrating event, team leaders expressed confidence that the robot would work well, because technical projections showed that it would be fast enough. However, Brian Kennedy from Targeted Convergence would not accept numbers on paper as a proof of feasibility. So the engineers set out to run 1,500 parts to prove there would not be a problem—and they discovered that the robot broke down after 80 parts! It took almost a year of trial, error, and improvement for problems with the robot arm to be resolved so that it worked as well in practice as it was supposed to work on paper.

The working group learned that feasibility meant the idea had to actually work in practice, so they started finding many ways to do extensive testing using available fixtures and silicon. As the year before first silicon progressed, everyone met weekly at a large progress board to discuss the status of each project. Gradually the projects began to be completed, and the 3X Working Group systematically drove out waste. There was a lot of cheap pre-silicon learning, and the teams gained confidence that they would avoid major delays, especially the expensive ones on the test floor. Morale was high and PDE engineers felt "incredibly ready" for first silicon to arrive.

First Silicon

To keep up with the anticipated demand for test software, the working group put in place a process that would deliver a new, validated test system every two weeks during the six-month drive to PRQ. Let's look at how it works (Figures 2-3 and 2-4).

The Platform   At the heart of the test system is an infrastructure and set of tools; you might think of this as the test platform. At the end of every second week, the teams that are responsible for this platform add a few new capabilities. Typically these teams are functional teams;

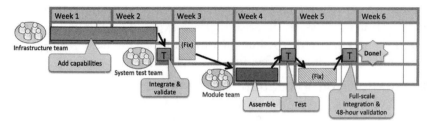

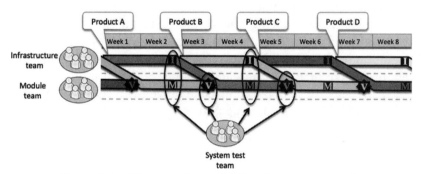

Figure 2-3   Five-week development cycle for one set of tests

Figure 2-4   New set of tests validated every two weeks

they focus on a specific technology area within the platform. Their work is integrated into the test system and validated by the system test team over the weekend. In the rare event that a problem occurs, it is fixed first thing the next week. Then the functional teams begin their next two-week iteration.

The Modules There are also cross-functional teams whose job it is to put together modules that assemble infrastructure and tools to test specific silicon configurations; you might think of modules as apps running on the platform. The module teams work in two-week iterations, offset by a week from the platform teams. Thus, module teams start a week after the platform teams complete a technology drop, giving the latest drop time to be validated and for any problems to be fixed.

The module teams have only a week to assemble (or modify) a module; the first weekend of the iteration is spent testing each module with short runs of silicon chips, and the early part of the second week is spent fixing any problems. As soon as all modules are solid and free of defects, the complete testing system is integrated and ready for its full-scale, 48-hour validation. Because of the extensive module-testing procedures, it is rare that module defects are found during final validation. However, issues do arise that are exposed by the volume testing, and they are addressed at the beginning of the next week before new module development begins.

Integration and Validation The integration team works in two-week cycles, with the bulk of their work focused on weekend integration and validation. On the first weekend they integrate the technology drop from the platform teams and also validate the new modules with short runs of silicon. On the second weekend they do a full-scale integration and run the 48-hour validation testing, with the robust robot arm doing its job of placing tens of thousands of chips in sockets so every aspect of the test can be validated. If any issues are found, the integration team works with the appropriate teams early the following week to resolve them. A root cause analysis of each problem is conducted and measures are put in place to prevent a recurrence. After all, the integration team is not supposed to find problems; it is supposed to *not* find problems.

Results

Things went extremely well when first silicon arrived. Capacity to deliver had indeed improved by a factor of three over two years earlier; in fact, it had improved much more when compared to the pre-agile days. The test success rate, already very good with agile development, increased another notch.

But something happened during the two-year cycle that caught PDE by surprise. Market conditions had prompted the addition of more products to the new-generation silicon than had originally been anticipated. So tripling productivity was not quite enough. By adding people and working longer hours, the PDE teams were able to keep up with the unexpectedly large workload, helped greatly by their rapid cadence and the rigorous validation regime.

Expanding across Intel

It took many years of continuous improvement for the Oregon PDE department to reach its current level, and there is no doubt that more improvement will follow. But PDE is just one small group of engineers in a very large company. The next step is to spread the learning through both high-level support and on-the-ground coaching. Intel is in the process of establishing both company-level and site-level agile competency centers to coordinate communities of practice and provide experienced coaches to support and accelerate adoption of the improved processes Intel needs as it continues its quest to keep up with Moore's Law and a rapidly changing market.

Otto: You would think that PDE has figured out most of the improvement that's possible. How can they keep on improving during the next cycle?

M&T: We don't know what PDE will do for the next cycle, but since Intel has been doing the seemingly impossible for decades, we assume they will figure something out. Intel is a company where you find the kind of engineers who are eager to be challenged and invent better ways of doing things.

The Science of Expertise

Think about musicians and athletes: How do they become virtuosos or champions? They practice. Decades of research, initiated by the work of Anders Ericsson, has led to consistent findings: Expertise is developed through hours upon hours of deliberate practice. What is deliberate practice? Think of those musicians and athletes. They

1. Decide to pursue a challenging goal
2. Practice under the guidance of a coach
3. Push their limits, fail, and receive immediate feedback
4. Repeat this over and over again, many times a day, for years

The elements necessary for organizational mastery are not much different. Excellent organizations that are masters in their field follow an equation something like this:

Expertise = Challenge + Coaching + Progress + Perseverance

Challenge

Some people are optimists. They pursue goals with enthusiasm; when asked to try something, their default answer is "Yes!" They take more risks, explore more options, and end up being more creative than their more pessimistic colleagues. Those pessimists, on the other hand, are more vigilant, more detail oriented, and less likely to make serious mistakes. When asked to try something new, their default answer would be "Is it safe?" There is certainly value in being paranoid; people who worry about making mistakes are careful, they value accuracy, and they don't let things slip between the cracks. You might think of optimists as people with a "can do" attitude and pessimists as those who believe that "failure is not an option." In the digital world, we tend to have the optimists developing software and the pessimists running the data centers—for good reason.

Columbia University researcher Troy Higgins would say that optimists are people with a **promotion focus**—they care about the presence and absence of gains—while pessimists are people with a **prevention focus**—they worry about the presence and absence of losses.[11] The focus people have at any point in time will depend on their goal. For example, an aspirational goal turns on a promotion focus in people—they become eager to work for the goal and are strongly motivated by progress. A goal that involves duties and obligations turns on the prevention focus in people—they become vigilant and are strongly motivated by a desire to avoid doing the wrong thing.

So which is better—promotion or prevention? Higgins has proposed what he calls the **Regulatory Fit Theory**. It says that people learn from a young age to favor one focus or the other, and they respond best to goals that most closely match their "chronic focus." In other words, some people are more motivated by pursuing opportunities and others are more motivated by preventing failure. It is best, Higgins's theory says, to give aspirational goals to people with a habitual promotion focus, while those with a chronic prevention focus will do better with goals focused on safety and security. Of course, this is not an absolute rule. When a child stands at the side of a road trying to decide whether to cross, you certainly hope she takes on a prevention focus and worries about safety. But once she is safely across the street, the child with an optimistic outlook is eager to explore more widely and willing to ignore the occasional setback.

The important thing to remember about regulatory fit is that for people who have a promotion focus, aspirations are strong motivators; for people who have a prevention focus, meeting obligations and fear of failure are strong motivators.

---

11. E. Troy Higgins, "Beyond Pleasure and Pain," *American Psychologist*, December 1977.

Goals for Pessimists

Let's review the Intel case study in the light of promotion and prevention focus. The Intel PDE group clearly has a prevention focus. After all, their job is to create the tests that qualify new products, so success means that bad products will always be detected. They work under tight time constraints to be sure, but above all else their job is to make sure that no defective chips get past their verification systems. This is a meaningful challenge.

Many people work in jobs that are primarily prevention focused: emergency workers and medical personnel, people who maintain our infrastructure, and those who protect our safety. Research has shown that prevention-focused challenges can be very motivating: reduce deaths due to infection; keep company data centers online 24/7; publish the newspaper every day in the face of unexpected disaster.[12] For these kinds of goals, setbacks are likely to inspire redoubled efforts rather than discourage people, because the overriding goal is not to fail. Quite surprisingly, praise tends to cause people pursuing prevention-focused goals to relax and perhaps not try as hard. When pursuing prevention-focused goals, constant vigilance is critically important and constantly getting better is what matters.

Goals for Optimists

Now let's look at the Intel case study from a different perspective. For a very long time, the overriding driver at Intel has been to keep up with Moore's Law—clearly a goal with a promotion focus, one that has been challenging designers for decades. This is the kind of challenge that inspires ingenuity and encourages people to investigate multiple options that might move their work to the next level. When you are looking for innovation, promotion-focused goals are the way to go. Even though Intel's PDE department is fundamentally prevention focused (its goal is to keep bad product from getting to market), it took on the challenge of tripling productivity—a promotion-focused goal—because that is the kind of improvement the company stands for.

---

12. See Heidi Grant Halvorson, *Succeed: How We Can Reach Our Goals* (Hudson Street Press, 2010), especially Chapter 4, "Goals for Optimists and Goals for Pessimists."

There is a theory of motivation called the Expectancy Value Theory, which says that when pursuing promotion-focused goals, motivation is a function of the likelihood of success (expectancy) and the size of the gain (value). So if the likelihood of success appears to diminish when pursuing aspirational goals, people are likely to get discouraged, because believing that success is within reach is critical to motivation. However, believing that success will be *easy* is an entirely different thing. If people think they will succeed without any hard work, they are likely to quit at the first sign that things are getting difficult. So the idea with promotion-focused goals is to make sure that people can see a path to success but understand that hard work will be required to get there.[13]

Framing the Challenge

By now you may be asking, "What is a good challenge? What does it look like?" First of all, decide how the challenge will be framed; is it a save-the-company-from-disaster challenge, or is it a move-the-company-to-the-next-level challenge? The two look quite different.

For prevention-focused—save-the-company-from-disaster—challenges, it is important for people to believe that the threat of failure is real, and they have to care. People tend to care about a company that cares about them, and when they believe the company they care about is threatened, they will rise to the challenge presented by the threat. So a prevention challenge calls on the people in the company to help it avoid mistakes (prevent any bad chips from getting out of the plant) or fend off competitive threats.

For promotion-focused—move-the-company-to-the-next-level—challenges, it is important that people consider the goal to be both meaningful and possible; it is also important for the goal to be difficult to reach. Too often a company pursues an easy, silver-bullet solution to a problem, but in fact, the perception that things should be easy causes people to become discouraged at the first sign of difficulty. So you want to look for a goal that, while achievable, will require a good deal of intelligence and ingenuity in order to be accomplished. At the same time, the goal should be one that people find meaningful, one they will be excited to pursue. Intel's pursuit of Moore's Law is a good example.

Can Regulatory Fit Cause Innovation Problems?

In general, the larger a company gets, the more it has to lose, and thus the more it tends to avoid risk. It seems that it is the nature of most

---

13. Ibid., Chapter 1.

large, publicly held companies to be chronically prevention focused; leaders tend to be motivated by a sense of responsibility to the company's many stakeholders and a fear of making mistakes. When these prevention-focused companies decide to take on a promotion-focused goal—innovation, for instance—there is a dissonance between the chronic safety focus of the organization and the aspirational goal of disruptive innovation. Making small improvements to existing products or processes is all that is encouraged.

Thus, one very likely cause of innovation problems in large companies is that the regulatory fit is wrong. These companies have developed a strong prevention focus, but significant innovation cries out for a promotion focus. The dissonance is deafening. Unless the prevention-focused company can internalize the very real threat of sticking with the status quo, isolated and timid innovation efforts might get started, but they are unlikely to thrive.

There are three approaches to deal with a regulatory fit problem:

1. Leaders at the top of the company change its regulatory fit (i.e., culture).
2. People in the company see the very real threat of failing to innovate and internalize the fact that innovation is a survival strategy.
3. The company splits into two camps: one with a chronic prevention focus and one with a habitual promotion focus.

The first option, changing the culture, is really hard. The second option, innovating because it is a survival issue, is somewhat easier. But the easiest approach is often to isolate innovation efforts in a separate organization where goals and metrics are promotion focused, which is more or less the equivalent of creating an internal startup company. We will discuss this further in Chapter 5.

Anna: Why does a challenge have to be meaningful to the workers? What's wrong with a goal that is meaningful to the company?

M&T: A challenge should absolutely be a goal that is meaningful to the company, but people have a hard time dedicating their heart and soul to goals such as increasing shareholder value. People are inspired by something they believe is important—doubling the computer power available to the world every two years (Intel) or working to help people be healthy (Merck).

Coaching

Consider a situation where leaders have a great strategy and workers are eager to execute it. What can go wrong? Just about everything. Having the right goals might get you 10% of the way toward achieving them, but not much more. What you have at that point is what Nilofer Merchant calls an **Air Sandwich**:

> An Air Sandwich is, in effect, a strategy that has a clear vision and future direction on the top layer, day-to-day action on the bottom, and virtually nothing in the middle—no meaty key decisions that connect the two layers, no rich chewy center filling to align the new direction with the new actions within the company.[14]

At Intel, PDE leaders realized that the 3X Working Group needed a lot more than a challenge to triple productivity. Group members needed to have this translated into actionable goals. They needed a disciplined process for reaching those goals. They needed a way to ensure cross-team learning. They needed visible status chats and progress checkpoints. They needed an outsider's perspective to teach the software folks that when you're dealing with hardware, calculations on paper aren't enough. They needed someone to notice that stuff was falling between the cracks and to create more projects around hidden dependencies. This was the meat between the high-level strategy and the efforts of the working group teams.

If you think of achieving mastery in your organization in the same terms as a musician or athlete, you know that for many years, you need a coach. There may come a time when you surpass all available coaches and take on the discipline of deliberate practice yourself, but that is far in the future for most mortals. Coaches, teachers, and mentors play a fundamental role in helping an organization achieve success.

But be careful, because institutionalizing the role of coach can get you in trouble. Far too often companies add a separate role of coach, a role without responsibility, rather than reconceive the roles of existing line managers and team leads as teachers and coaches. Companies that add a coach to an existing reporting structure often find that the coach and line manager have more or less the same job, so one of them is redundant—and that would probably *not* be the line manager.

---

14. Nilofer Merchant, *The New How: Building Business Solutions through Collaborative Strategy* (O'Reilly Media, 2009).

Think of coaches as the people who can distill a large amount of learning from their experience and guide organizations that are just getting started in the right direction. If they are wise, they will focus much of their effort on transferring their knowledge to local leaders, who then become the ongoing coaches for their organization.

 Otto: Are you saying that work teams don't need a coach?
M&T: Indeed, teams need a coach. But we're saying that the coach will often be the existing manager; in fact, being a coach should be a key part of a manager's job.

Progress

"Truly effective videogame designers know how to create a sense of progress for players within all stages of a game. Truly effective managers know how to do the same for their teams," according to Teresa Amabile and Steven Kramer.[15] A few years ago, they set out to study what motivates knowledge workers. They had knowledge workers (such as engineers and programmers) in several companies keep diaries of their work life, recording what they were thinking every day. After analyzing thousands of diary entries, they came to the conclusion that the biggest motivator for knowledge workers on a day-to-day basis is *making progress in meaningful work.*

This sounds pretty obvious, right? But consider this. Amabile and Kramer asked over 600 managers to rank the importance of five factors for motivating employees: recognition, incentives, interpersonal support, support for making progress, and clear goals. The managers ranked *recognition* first and *support for making progress* dead last.[16] What do you think would have happened if they had asked the same question of music teachers? Martial arts instructors? Athletic coaches? Research advisers? These kinds of mentors learned long ago that people will work hard day after day as long as they *keep getting better*, keep making progress. They know that occasional recognition is a good thing, interpersonal support helps, clear goals must be paired

15. Teresa Amabile and Steven Kramer, *The Progress Principle: Using Small Wins to Ignite Joy, Engagement, and Creativity at Work* (Harvard Business Review Press, 2011).
16. Teresa M. Amabile and Steven J. Kramer, "What Really Motivates Workers," in "The HBR List: Breakthrough Ideas for 2010," *Harvard Business Review*, January 2010.

with feedback, and incentives are poison. And they realize that none of these factors will keep students motivated over time unless they experience steady progress.

The motivational power of progress, well known in just about every field that focuses on mastery, seems to have been lost on most managers. But it makes sense. This is why it is a good idea to break large goals (3X productivity increase) into small goals (demonstrated ability to add six features to XYZ test every two weeks) and make progress visible. Don't think of measuring progress as a control mechanism; think of it as a motivation mechanism and you will create a completely different atmosphere.

> **Anna:** So are all those progress charts we like to see a good thing?
>
> **M&T:** Absolutely! Visible tools that facilitate discussions about what's going on and what needs to be done to keep things on track are great. In fact, daily or weekly meetings around visible progress charts have been used for decades in many business settings as a way of keeping progress visible while keeping team members synchronized and committed to each other.

Perseverance

In a comparative study of perseverance in Japan and North America,[17] Steven Heine and his colleagues found that culture has a lot of influence on what motivates people to persevere at challenging tasks. In North America in particular, and Western cultures in general, people tend to persevere in working on tasks that they are good at. Failure tends to cause them to abandon a task. In Japan, and by extension in other East Asian cultures, they found the opposite—failure tends to increase motivation and cause people to work harder. By now you might have guessed the reason behind this. The researchers note that North Americans tend to have a promotion focus—they are likely to pursue gains—while a Japanese heritage tends to value a prevention focus—a focus on living up to expectations.

 Let's take a closer look at the North American/Western tendency to get discouraged as a result of failure. We know that failure does not necessarily discourage people

---

17. Steven J. Heine et al., "Divergent Consequences of Success and Failure in Japan and North America: An Investigation of Self-Improving Motivations and Malleable Selves," *Journal of Personality and Social Psychology* 81, no. 4 (2001): 599–615.

with aspirational goals. Musicians, for instance, know that if they spend their practice time performing perfectly, they are wasting their time. So they spend hours each day pushing the limits, making mistakes, and learning from them. So do competitive athletes; similarly, people pursuing martial arts. But in most of these pursuits, progress is rewarded by reaching the next level, not by comparing individuals to each other. Everyone understands that the way to reach the next level is with practice, and it doesn't matter that some will reach the next level more quickly than others. You will reach the next level when you have practiced hard enough to get there.

When we rank people against each other rather than recognize their current level of accomplishment, we are not doing their motivation any favors. Yet Western cultures seem to have a great need to give children grades and force adults into a slightly skewed bell curve at work. So school and work are not practice times where we are expected to push the limits and make mistakes; all that does is get us a lower grade or rating. You have to wonder why Western cultures think ranking people against each other is so useful, despite plenty of evidence that says otherwise.[18]

A meaningful and challenging goal is inspiring—for example, earn a black belt in Taekwondo. And intermediate short-term goals—color belts—are motivating. But the thing that has to happen day in and day out is practice, practice, practice. People must find constant practice and steady improvement engaging in order to persevere.

 Anna: So if we don't rank people, what do we do?
M&T: The best promotion systems are level systems, as opposed to ranking systems. Each job title or level is defined by a job description that describes what is required to be promoted to that level. Typically a higher level entails more independent work, responsibility to direct the work of others, and so on. As long as people are not in competition with their peers for promotion—as long as a promotion is an indication that the person is performing at the next level and people can expect to get promoted when they have earned it—promotion systems can work very well.

Otto: I've seen many people become experts, only to have others refuse to trust their expertise. How do you know when someone is really an expert?

---

18. See in particular Jeffrey Pfeffer and Robert Sutton, "Evidence-Based Management," *Harvard Business Review*, January 2006.

M&T: That's a good question. There is quite a controversy these days over whether or not you can trust the intuition, or expertise, of others. Let's take a closer look at the issues.

When Can We Trust Intuition?

There's an interesting debate going on in the world of psychology about how to know if you can trust an expert. On the one hand, Daniel Kahneman has spent decades devising experiments that demonstrate cognitive biases—ways that our intuition tricks us into making less than optimal decisions. On the other hand, Gary Klein has spent his career studying experts at work in crisis-prone jobs, and he concludes that for many jobs, it is critically important to develop and rely on expert intuition. It took these two leaders in the field of intuition and decision-making seven years to find enough common ground to write a joint paper in which they tried to agree on an answer to the question *Under what conditions are the intuitions of professionals worthy of trust?*[19] Let's take a quick tour of their work and their conclusions.

Cognitive Biases

Daniel Kahneman and Amos Tversky began investigating how intuition works in 1969. Their experiments showed that in complex situations, intuition doesn't work very well, but our fast-thinking minds make judgments anyway, introducing biases into our decisions. Exposing these intuition biases, or cognitive biases, dealt a death blow to the theory that most people make rational decisions most of the time. In 2002 Kahneman won the Nobel Prize in Economics for this work.[20]

Kahneman's book *Thinking, Fast and Slow* is the story of our two modes of thinking—System 1 and System 2—which we discussed in the Introduction. To recap, System 1, or fast thinking, is our intuition at work; in most situations, intuition uses a set of shortcuts, norms, averages, or patterns to evaluate the situation and come to conclusions. If we detect that these conclusions aren't good enough, we switch to System 2, or slow thinking, do our homework, look at the evidence, calculate, and make rational choices.

---

19. Daniel Kahneman and Gary Klein, "Conditions for Intuitive Expertise: A Failure to Disagree," *American Psychologist* 64, no. 6 (September 2009): 515–26.
20. Tversky would no doubt have shared the prize, but he died in 1996.

The problem is, our slow-thinking self is lazy, so we use fast thinking as often as possible. We don't really want to know about all of the alternatives that might be available; we would rather just let our fast-thinking mode handle the situation. Actually, this is necessary, because we don't have the energy to make every decision—or even most decisions—in the slow-thinking mode. But the problem is, according to Kahneman, that we don't recognize the biases of intuition that influence our fast-thinking self, even when we are aware that these biases exist.

Cognitive biases make learning difficult, because they make failure hard to detect. We are strongly biased to believe that whatever path we have chosen is the best path and are unlikely to waver in our pursuit of our chosen goal, even if it is clear to others that it is the wrong goal. We are biased to ignore criticism and to be blind to our own failings, even though we are keenly aware of failings in other people.

In theory, evidence-based decisions should overcome our cognitive biases. But gathering and examining the evidence requires slow thinking, and slow thinking is hard work, so we try to avoid it. And even when we do examine the evidence, if it contradicts what we expect, our confirmation bias is likely to kick in and explain it away. So even gathering data and doing analysis is not a guarantee that our cognitive biases will be put aside and objective decisions will be made.

Dealing with Cognitive Biases

In the book *Decisive*, Chip and Dan Heath provide a wide range of techniques to deal with cognitive biases.[21] First off, they suggest, important decisions should be approached with an array of options. If you find yourself asking, "Should we or shouldn't we?" you have narrowed your options to a single choice. If you are making an "either/or" decision, you have limited your options to only two choices. This is the way teenagers are likely to make decisions, according to the Heaths; it is hardly a good way for high-impact corporate decisions to be made.

Look for additional options, even options that seem less attractive than the most favored choices. Don't write off the undesirable options; ask instead, "What would we have to believe in order for these options to be a good choice?" Or ask, "What if *none* of the options we are considering were available; *then* what would we do?"

---

21. Chip Heath and Dan Heath, *Decisive: How to Make Better Choices in Life and Work* (Crown Business, 2013).

In addition to broadening your options, the Heaths recommend that you reality-test your assumptions by running quick experiments and inviting disagreement. They suggest that you step back from the situation and look at it from a distance. Finally, if you are going down a path where most travelers fail—say you are starting a new business—accept the fact that your chances of failure are the same as the chances of those who have gone before you. So it's a good idea to be prepared to be wrong.

Expert Intuition

Gary Klein appreciates that research into cognitive biases has revealed important truths about the way our minds work, but he does not agree with Kahneman's distrust of intuition. He points out that Kahneman's experiments were done in artificial settings with novices working through controlled scenarios. Klein studied people in unpredictable situations where life-and-death decisions must be made quickly—firefighters, nurses, military personnel. He has compared the responses of novices and experts and marvels at the amazing ability of experts to make superb decisions in difficult situations. He concludes that training and experience should be used to expose novices to scenarios where their intuition fails so they can learn from their mistakes and increase their expertise.

So how do experts use their intuition to make decisions? According to Klein, the first question experienced firefighters ask when they arrive at a fire is not *What do I do?* It is *What's going on?* They have rich mental models of various fire situations, and they look for a pattern that is similar to the current situation. When they find a pattern that matches, it presents them with an option of what to do. They run a quick scenario in their minds to see how that option is likely to play out, and if it looks good, they go with that option. Then they monitor the situation to see if the scenario is working and reassess if it is not. Finally, after the emergency is past, they replay the situation and learn from any mistakes, which further enriches their mental model.

Klein tells the story of a lieutenant leading a crew fighting a kitchen fire.[22] The fire didn't respond the way it should have—something felt wrong—so he ordered everyone to get out of the building. Just after they left, the floor they had been standing on collapsed into a flaming

---

22. Gary Klein, *Sources of Power: How People Make Decisions* (The MIT Press, 1998), Example 4.1.

basement. How did the lieutenant know that something was wrong? He had years of experience observing fire patterns and had built a rich mental model of the various ways in which a house burns. This fire did not match any patterns in his mental model. He realized he did not understand what was going on and became uncomfortable being in the house. So he had everyone get out—just in time.

When less experienced people make decisions in equally difficult situations, they use the same approach. But without a rich mental model of the situation, they have limited options to choose from, limited ability to see potential problems while imagining the scenario, and limited ability to detect when the scenario is not going well. The best way to train these novices is to help them to build a rich mental model of the domain by using mentors and simulations.

A good way to make sure that novices do *not* develop into experts, according to Klein, is to expect them to follow standard procedures so that they never make a mistake. For complex, urgent, threatening situations it is much safer to teach people how to recover from mistakes than to focus on making sure that they never make a mistake in the first place. Gary Klein says, "We put too much emphasis on reducing errors and not enough on building expertise."[23]

Anna: So you're saying if I want to be comfortable that the right decisions are being made, I need people with a rich mental model of the situation?

M&T: That is correct. And you have to make sure those people are in a position to use their expertise to make decisions and guide actions.

Anna: But how do I know which experts to trust?

M&T: Gary Klein and Daniel Kahneman agree that the kind of expertise that can be trusted is built in a relatively constrained environment that provides decision makers with reliable feedback about the results of their decisions.[24] For example, emergency room doctors will be good at making decisions about emergency medical situations, but often they have not built up the expertise to make long-term diagnoses, since they usually do not follow their patients over time to see if their diagnoses are correct.

---

23. Gary Klein, *Streetlights and Shadows: Searching for the Keys to Adaptive Decision Making* (The MIT Press, 2009), p. 13.
24. Kahneman and Klein, "Conditions for Intuitive Expertise."

Resiliency

What does developing expertise look like in practice? A good example can be found in the discussion "Resilience Engineering: Learning to Embrace Failure."[25] In this article, Jesse Robbins discusses how his firefighter training led him to convince his company (Amazon.com) that the best way to keep their complex systems up and running was not to make them perfect, but to make them resilient. In order to do this, he started GameDay events—events that are triggered by intentionally pulling the plug on a data center (or a similar self-inflicted failure). For a typical GameDay event, it may take dozens of people two or three days to get the system back to normal. Once things are working again, a detailed review occurs in which dependencies and process weaknesses exposed by the exercise are documented and most of them are rapidly fixed. In addition, the people involved in responding to the emergency use the feedback to build their expertise.

Resiliency is built over time by breaking things in order to find latent problems and learn how to recover from the inevitable failures that every complex system harbors. This kind of testing reveals everything from very tough problems to simple oversights. Quite a few problems originate in the product development process, so the learning from a single event can move a long way back into the company to change everything from design standards to testing approaches.

Other companies with very large data centers—Google, for example—hold similar events. Over time, these exercises have created the learning, confidence, and resilience that allow companies to be comfortable with massive complexity. There is no thought of perfection; it is simply impossible. There is no thought of declaring victory; learning through failure injection is a never-ending journey of constantly getting better. People grow in expertise and gain confidence in their ability to handle the confusion of an outage, and the company's systems and processes become more hardened against catastrophe.

The Paradox of Perfection

 Initially, failure injection events were very hard to sell. The prevailing wisdom was that data centers should not fail; they were measured by the percentage of uptime they could guarantee—and it was supposed to approach 100%. It was

25. A discussion with Jesse Robbins, Kripa Krishnan, John Allspaw, and Tom Limoncelli, "Resilience Engineering: Learning to Embrace Failure," *Communications of the ACM*, November 2012.

thought that excellent data centers were the ones that were able to eliminate downtime; it seemed inappropriate for data centers to spend time worrying about how fast they could recover from failures that were not supposed to happen. Intentionally causing a failure—one that could have serious consequences—is actually quite risky. And it is also expensive; these exercises involve many people working around the clock for days.

Companies that pursue resiliency through failure injection have come to understand two basic facts:

1. Perfection is impossible in a complex system at scale. No matter how low the probability of a failure is, the number of transactions is so large that the only real question is when, not if, a failure will happen.

2. It is a lot less expensive to develop the expertise to recover quickly and safely from failure than it is to pretend that failure will not happen.

It can take a radical cultural shift for a company to accept the idea that perfection is not the right goal; resilience is a much better goal in the context of complexity. And resiliency is built on, and builds, expertise.

Questions to Ponder

1. Appraisal and compensation practices seem to come in two flavors. One flavor supports a mindset that assumes talent is a fixed asset in a person. The other flavor supports a growth mindset that assumes talent can be significantly increased through hard work and experience. Looking honestly and critically at the practices in your company, which mindset do they reflect?

2. If you consider the output of your product development practices over time, do you see a steady improvement, or do people become relatively satisfied after a single successful change? Why? What are you doing/can you do to maintain steady progress?

3. If you were to choose a single challenge that would inspire people in your organization to do their best work, what would it be?

4. What is the role of a coach or mentor in your organization? If you could redesign the role from scratch, would it be different?

5. Do you have practices in place that create a sense of steady progress for workers? How are they working? How do you know?

6. Do your organization's metrics and practices reflect a bias toward quick fixes or challenging long-term goals?

7. What is the role of expertise in your company? How is it developed? Are internal experts trusted? Do external experts have a higher status?

8. Does your company have a process to counteract cognitive biases in decision making? How well does it work? How could it be improved?

9. In what circumstances would failure injection be a good idea in your world?

10. What percentage of the people in your organization would you categorize as "energized"? What practices are in place to engage and energize workers?

3
Delighted Customers

> The Westerner and the Japanese mean something different when they talk of "making a decision." With us in the West, all the emphasis is on the *answer* to the question. . . . To the Japanese, however, the important element in decision-making is *defining the question.*[1]
>
> —Peter Drucker

Ask the Right Questions

The Internet may be the platform that launched the information age, but a century earlier, the internal combustion engine was the platform that launched the transportation age. Reset your clock to the 1890s, and you will see numerous automobile companies trying to sort out what the automobile would eventually become. You will discover people attaching engines to balloons trying to figure out what kind of air travel was possible. And you will find a few intrepid inventors dreaming of flying machines that were heavier than air and could fly like birds.

Learning to Fly

One of the dreamers was Otto Lilienthal, a German engineer who built and flew gliders, logging over 2,000 glider flights. He published a highly

---

1. Peter F. Drucker, "What We Can Learn from Japanese Management," *Harvard Business Review*, March–April 1971. Emphasis added. Used with permission.

influential book, *Birdflight as the Basis of Aviation*,[2] which contained detailed information on wing shapes and measurements of lift, before his untimely death in a glider crash in 1896. Another aviation pioneer was the French-born American engineer Octave Chanute, who designed and tested gliders on the windy southern shores of Lake Michigan. And then there was the Secretary of the Smithsonian Institution, Samuel Pierpont Langley, who outfitted a scale-model glider with a steam engine and got it to fly for over a kilometer in 1896. But when he scaled up his design in 1903 to a human-size glider, it crashed ingloriously into the Potomac River. Luckily the pilot could swim.

Meanwhile in Dayton, Ohio, a couple of bicycle shop proprietors, brothers Wilbur and Orville Wright, were inspired by these pioneers and decided that gliding would be an interesting hobby.[3] They studied all the material they could get their hands on, and eventually Wilbur concluded: "You can reduce this problem to three basic systems. If you are going to invent an airplane you have to have wings that are going to generate lift, you got to have a propulsion system that will move the wings through the air and you got to have a way to control the wings once you're in the air. Lift aerodynamics, propulsion, and control—that's it."[4]

The Wright brothers realized that the most overlooked flight system was neither the lift aerodynamics nor the propulsion system; it was the control system. They asked a question that was being ignored by almost everyone else; rather than ask, *How do we fly?* they asked, *How do we keep from falling out of the sky?* They decided it would be safest to start by solving the control problem.

In particular, the Wright brothers investigated ways to control the lateral motion, or roll, of an airplane. Most land vehicles do not need lateral control—it is provided by four wheels resting on the ground—so most of the aviation pioneers did not consider lateral stability to be a problem, or if they did, they could not imagine how to deal with it. On the other hand, bicycles do have a lateral stability problem that must

---

2. Otto Lilienthal, *Birdflight as the Basis of Aviation*, published in German in 1889.
3. See Orville Wright, *How We Invented the Airplane: An Illustrated History*, ed. Fred C. Kelly, first published in 1953 from text written in 1920. Republished with new material in 1988 by Dover Publications, Inc.
4. From a talk that Tom Crouch (Senior Curator of Aeronautics at the National Air and Space Museum of the Smithsonian Institution) gave on August 19, 2007, at the Wright Brothers National Memorial, Kill Devil Hills, NC, http://wrightstories.com/tom-crouch-talks-wright-brothers/.

be taken into account in the design of the bike. So it's not a surprise that a couple of bicycle mechanics realized that the critical problem in aircraft design was controlling the roll of the plane.

Glider pilots controlled roll by shifting their weight, but this was not going to work with powered flight, and it clearly wasn't working very well for gliders either. Upon reflection, the Wright brothers came up with the idea of controlling lateral motion with wing warping (dynamically changing the shape of the wings). In 1899 they built a large kite to test this idea and it seemed to work well. In 1900 they built a glider that incorporated wing warping, using the Lilienthal tables of air pressure and a bi-wing design from Chanute.

 Wilbur and Orville Wright searched for a windy place to test their glider and settled on the Outer Banks of North Carolina. They transported their glider from Dayton and set up camp near Kitty Hawk, expecting to be able to glide for hours at a time in the costal winds. They were disappointed; the glider would not lift unless the winds were very strong, and it did not stay in the air very long. However, when it did fly, the lateral control worked rather well. They did a series of experiments gliding down a nearby hill called Kill Devil Hill to try to find out what was wrong with their design.

The Wright brothers wrote to Chanute to ask for advice, and he suggested that their wing design needed to more closely match Lilienthal's. So they decided to build another glider over the winter, but when they tested it in 1901, they found it was a step backward. They modified the wing shape and got some improvement, but after several hundred flights they were very discouraged. Finally they came to ask their second key question: *Are the accepted aerodynamic design tables right? Is the coefficient of lift that has been around for 100 years correct?*

Wilbur and Orville Wright didn't have the time or money to build more gliders, so they devised an experiment carried out on a bicycle to prove to themselves that the published data was wrong. Then they asked themselves, *Can we generate the data we need—here in our bike shop over the winter?* They built a simple wooden wind tunnel that allowed them to test multiple configurations of airfoils against each other. In the winter of 1901–2, the Wright brothers carefully ran thousands of experiments; by the end of the winter they had developed a revised body of knowledge about aerodynamic lift.

With the problem correctly framed and valid data in hand, the Wright brothers knew what kind of wing shapes and angles would work best. The glider they built in 1902 worked remarkably well, with its lift matching predictions. As they flew the glider, the brothers realized that when turning in crosswinds, controlling the roll of the plane (rotation around the front-to-back axis) was not enough; they also needed to control yaw (rotation around the vertical axis), so they added a vertical rudder. By fall, Wilbur and Orville Wright knew they had solved the most important problem facing glider flight—the control problem—and they had made major advances in solving the lift problem as well. It's worth noting that their control approach and wing designs are used in aircraft design to this day.

However, if they were going to glide in the air for hours, the brothers knew that an engine would be needed. So they asked, *What kind of engine and propeller would we need to change the glider into a flier?* Wind tunnel experiments showed that a light engine that could produce at least 8 horsepower would be adequate. They could not get an engine manufacturer to build such an engine at a price they could afford, so they worked with their bicycle shop mechanic, Charlie Taylor, to build an engine themselves. The simple engine was made of aluminum, a novel material at the time. It produced 12 horsepower—more than enough for flight. The next step was to design a propeller, so it was back to the wind tunnel to find the best shape. The resulting propeller ended up being one of the most efficient propellers of its day. The propellers were connected to the motor with bicycle chains, and *voilà!* A powered glider (the Wright Flyer) was ready to take off.

The Flyer was assembled and tested at the oceanside camp in the fall of 1903. After many experiments and propeller repairs, the brothers finally flew the Flyer in controlled flight on December 17. Orville and Wilbur each flew the Flyer twice; the longest flight lasted about a minute and covered about a quarter of a kilometer. At that point the Flyer was caught by heavy wind and destroyed.

Orville and Wilbur Wright returned home knowing that they had solved the basic problems of heavier-than-air flight. They built Flyer II and tested it the next year at Huffman Prairie, a field near their home in Dayton. It was underpowered and difficult to control, but by late 1905 the brothers had learned enough to redesign the aircraft again. Flyer III worked much better than its two predecessors; it might be called the first practical airplane.

After that, airplane development proceeded rapidly both in the United States and in Europe. In 1919, a mere 16 years after the first flight, an airplane was able to fly nonstop across the Atlantic Ocean.

Anna: I am impressed by the amount of analysis the Wright brothers did and the effort they went through to gather all that data. Was there anything in their education or background that explains why they did all of that analysis?

M&T: The Wright brothers had been encouraged from childhood to read widely and learn as much as possible, but their formal education ended after high school. They ran a print shop and then a bicycle shop, which fueled their love of books and gave them a lot of practical mechanical experience. The brothers were passionate about flying and considered it a hobby, so they dedicated all of their spare time to learning everything they could about it.

Otto: It's interesting to see how the mechanical experience of the Wright brothers gave them the intuition to ask the right questions.

M&T: One of the things that drove the brothers to ask the right questions was that they didn't have a lot of money, so they couldn't afford the random trial-and-error experiments that were common at the time. (This is an example of the conventional wisdom that constraints tend to drive innovation.) The Wright brothers tried to learn as much as they possibly could before they built anything. We like to call this **learn-first development**.[5] It's an important approach when every learning cycle is costly and takes a long time.

Solve the Right Problems

Customers never buy a product; they buy **the satisfaction of a want**, according to Peter Drucker. He wrote:

> True marketing starts out . . . with the customer, his demographics, his realities, his needs, his values. It does not ask, "What do we have to sell?" It asks, "What does the customer want to buy?" It does not say, "This is what our product or service does." It says, "These are the satisfactions the customer looks for, values, and needs." . . . The aim of marketing is to know and understand the customer so well that the product or service fits him and sells itself.[6]

---

5. This is the approach recommended by Michael Kennedy in *Ready, Set, Dominate* (Oaklea Press, 2008), and it is widely used in hardware product development.
6. Peter Drucker was introduced in Chapter 1. This quote is from *Management*.

Drucker was not alone in this view. Harvard Business School professor Theodore Levitt often told his students, "People don't want to buy a quarter-inch drill. They want a quarter-inch hole!" In his classic article "Marketing Myopia,"[7] Levitt wrote, ". . . the entire corporation must be viewed as a customer-creating and customer-satisfying organism."

In that article, Levitt observed that some companies "are in the felicitous position of having to fill, not find, markets, of not having to discover what the customer needs and wants but of having the customer voluntarily come forward with specific new product demands." He goes on to say that this situation is actually not such a good deal after all, because if scientists and engineers simply depend on customers to tell them what products to deliver, it is unlikely that they will develop a customer-oriented viewpoint.

How can this be? How can delivering what customers ask for be a bad thing? The problem, Levitt explains, is that if the development organization delivers exactly what customers ask for—a drill, for example—they will learn nothing about the kinds of holes the customer needs, what problem the holes are solving, and whether there might be a better way to address that problem. In fact, focusing on what existing customers are asking for is exactly what leads companies to ignore new, disruptive technologies until it's too late, as we will discuss further in Chapter 5.

What Are Requirements?

 Many engineers, particularly software engineers, are under the impression that their work should start out with a list of requirements (or perhaps a backlog of stories) that come from someone else. But a detailed list of requirements is not the starting point for good engineering. The Wright brothers did not start with requirements; they started out with an idea: Build a glider and learn to fly it and then add power (and don't get killed in the process). When they asked Charlie Taylor to build an engine, the "requirements" were the constraints imposed by the laws of physics: a weight limit and a horsepower minimum. Everything else was design.

The Wright brothers did not have enough money to waste effort on solving the wrong problems. They dove into deeply complex technical

---

7. Theodore Levitt, "Marketing Myopia," *Harvard Business Review*, July–August 1960.

problems with fearless vigor and amazingly disciplined attention to detail. They tackled the three flight systems one at a time. First they designed a control system—to keep from crashing; then they studied lift aerodynamics in detail and learned how to design the wings. Only after those two problems were solved did they add a propulsion system. This methodical approach enabled them to solve three extremely demanding technical problems in three years.

Great problem solvers start by developing a deep understanding of the situation through direct experience. They collaborate with people who have different perspectives and knowledge. They are creative, efficient, and highly disciplined in uncovering the essential problems and designing possible solutions. They test multiple ideas and focus on learning as much as they can. They ask a lot of questions and challenge assumptions, even their own assumptions. They regularly step back and reframe the situation to be sure they are solving the right problem.

If you are an entrepreneur today, you probably proceed more or less in this fashion. But if you are in a big company or a government department, you probably do not approach the development of a difficult system as a design problem; you are more likely to see it as an execution problem or a project management problem. But proceeding with a solution absent a good understanding of the underlying problem is all too often a recipe for disaster.

Case: The FBI Case Management System

The FBI Case Management System debacle—no, make that plural: debacles—have been blamed on many things. A decade of pouring buckets of money down the drain with nothing to show for it generates many excuses. From 2001 to 2004, $170 million was wasted before the Virtual Case File System was discarded. So what happened next? They tried again, forgetting Einstein's admonition that insanity is doing the same thing and expecting different results. The second fiasco was called Sentinel. Jerome Israel, the FBI's Chief Technical Officer from 2004 to 2009, published an article in *IEEE Computer* about just what went wrong.[8]

Israel noted that in 2005, the RFP (request for proposal) team was too busy generating requirements to build prototypes that would help

---

8. Jerome Israel, "Why the FBI Can't Build a Case Management System," *IEEE Computer* 45, no. 6 (June 2012).

clarify the most challenging technical issues. The reason was not simply a lack of time; the RFP team—and the FBI in general—did not have the engineering strength to really understand the nature of the problems that needed to be solved. Responses to the RFP showed that vendors had also failed to engage in really understanding the complexity of the system. In his article, Israel listed three "wicked" problems that an FBI case management system must resolve, problems that were not clearly understood or adequately addressed throughout the failed development effort. First of all there was a deeply complex access security problem that defied definition, let alone resolution. Second, there was a tricky migration problem, because a big-bang cutover was clearly not going to work. Third, there was every intention to use commercial off-the-shelf software, but integrating these disparate systems was "wicked hard," according to Israel.

To compensate for its lack of engineering skill, the FBI decided to emphasize program management. Program managers with no technical background were put in positions senior to government engineers who might understand the technical problems. The project management approach focused on tracking activity, not on making sure that the difficult technical problems were uncovered and addressed.

A contract for the Sentinel project was signed in March 2006 with delivery scheduled for December 2009. After 18 months Phase 1 was delivered, a Web-based interface to existing systems. Phase 2 would be the really difficult phase, so an iterative delivery approach was adopted. This would seem to be a good idea, but due to pressure to show regular progress, the focus of development turned toward the easy stuff; the really serious engineering that needed to be done was put aside. In October 2009, after two years of favorable progress reports, the wicked problems finally had to be faced. And, as Israel wrote, "all of the problems—[the wicked problems]—came crashing down on the project." A second disaster loomed.

In September 2010 a new FBI CTO, Jeff Johnson, halted the project and took over direct management of development. He assembled a small, technically competent team and housed it in a room in the basement of the FBI building. Using the techniques of software startups—agile practices, rapid delivery, and fast consumer-to-developer feedback loops—the team delivered a successful system two years later, at a cost of less than 5% of the sum that had been consumed by earlier attempts.

This is not a new story—except maybe the ending. For many years everything seemed to be going well, and then the project suddenly crashed—twice. Israel notes that after the first disaster, auditors decided the cause of the problem was lack of strong program management. So the second attempt had strong program managers, certified through an eight-week certification class or a nine-day boot camp. But that didn't work, because the root cause of the problem, according to Israel, was the absence of engineering leaders on the program to identify and make sure that progress was being made on the essential—wicked—technical problems. Instead, program managers, who had no idea what the critical technical issues were, used graphs and charts to show steady progress. On the wrong problems.

> **Anna:** That was quite the disaster. Why didn't the auditors figure out what went wrong the first time?
> **M&T:** The auditors found something that appeared to be wrong—the management of the project. Unfortunately, this wasn't the root cause of the problem. Israel wrote, "If Congress appropriates, say, $40 million a year for an IT program, no agency can capably dispose of that funding if it lacks engineering vision, experience, and skill." This was not what the auditors were looking for.

Don't Separate Design from Implementation

Coauthor Mary's first job was working on AT&T's Electronic Switching System (ESS). The first day on the job, she was told, "Our design goal for ESS is a maximum downtime of 15 minutes in 40 years." Mary observed that every person involved in development knew about that goal, and virtually every technical decision made at all levels supported the goal. AT&T's Electronic Switching System was one of the best-known examples of **Design by Objectives**, a popular design approach at the time.

The idea behind Design by Objectives is to define system objectives with a few high-level, measurable goals and then charter the engineers developing the system to design the detailed features and functions of the system so as to meet its high-level objectives. In effect, the high-level goals frame the customers' needs in a way that allows engineers at all levels to think creatively about those needs and investigate multiple ways to satisfy customers. This method was popularized by Tom Gilb in the book *Principles of Software Engineering Management.*[9]

---

9. Tom Gilb, *Principles of Software Engineering Management* (Pearson Education, originally published in Great Britain in 1988). Now in its twentieth printing.

Gilb, one of the earliest advocates of evolutionary development, has long advocated an exploratory approach to software development, with design decisions made based on how well a design contributes to meeting the high-level system objectives. Gilb has been pleased to see agile software development reaffirm the importance of evolutionary development, but he feels that agile development missed a key concept behind Design by Objectives. A development team, Gilb contends, should be given a short list of measurable outcomes (perhaps a dozen), the end goals of the system. These are the objectives that constrain the design of the system. The development team, interacting with customers, should design a solution that meets those objectives. They should *not* be given a set of detailed requirements. Gilb recently wrote:

> The worst scenario I can imagine is when we allow real customers, users, and our own salespeople to dictate "functions and features" to the developers, carefully disguised as "customer requirements." Maybe conveyed by our Product Owners. If you go slightly below the surface of these false "requirements" ("means," not "ends"), you will immediately find that they are not really requirements. They are really bad amateur design, for the "real" requirements. . . .[10]

The people who create the detailed requirements for a system are, in fact, designing the system itself. If they are not expert system designers, the system is being designed by amateurs. That's what happened in the FBI case. No amount of excellent program management could compensate for a design (i.e., set of requirements) that failed to consider the wicked problems of the system.

 Anna: Are you saying that there shouldn't be any requirements? What is the alternative? Should people just dive in and start doing things without any analysis or design? I don't see how that can work.

M&T: Think about it this way. The first step in developing a complex system is to be sure that the right questions are being asked, the right problems are being solved. The purpose of starting with design objectives is to frame the problem correctly and allow experts to investigate solutions to that problem. Starting with a long list of detailed "requirements" is jumping to a solution before taking

---

10. Tom Gilb, "Value-Driven Development Principles and Values," *Agile Record*, July 2010.

time to understand the problem. It is better to think of requirements as the few essential outcomes that are truly *required*. Detailed specifications will be developed in due time by people with appropriate expertise, but they are not the place to start.

 Otto: It seems to me that these days the most amazing products are things like smartphones and tablets and social media, and I'll bet they don't start out as a list of requirements.

M&T: You're right—it's hard to describe user experience as a list of requirements. When experience is important, the place to start is to develop a deep understanding of the targeted consumers, the job they might want a product to do for them, how they do that job now, what annoys them, and what might delight them.

Design a Compelling Experience

Thirty years ago, the mobile phone was a technical marvel, even though from a consumer perspective it was a brick. For over two decades, when mobile phone companies chose which problem to solve next, they usually selected technical problems that customers complained about: *Make the battery smaller. Put a full keyboard on the phone. Increase the resolution of the screen.*

Then with the release of the iPhone in 2007, mobile phone companies discovered that technology was no longer the most important issue. Competitive differentiation had shifted from technical features to the experience of using the phone. Suddenly the question to ask had become *How can we get customers to* love *our phone?*

Let's face it, competitive differentiation for a lot of products has shifted from engineering to design. For the most part, people are no longer amazed by the technical features of new products; they are amazed by great experiences. And when one of the key objectives of a system is to provide an amazing experience, the leadership of the product team should include an experienced designer.

 Designers are intuitive thinkers. They are trained to ask a lot of questions and generate a lot of ideas; they create designs—never just one design—by building a lot of quick prototypes to test out a range of possibilities. They focus on the kinds of emotions their designs will elicit. They constantly ask the question *What will make consumers love this product?*

There is a new executive position at many large companies these days: Chief Design Officer. Companies such as Procter & Gamble, 3M, Philips Electronics, GE Healthcare, Kia Motors, PepsiCo, Apple Computer, Whirlpool, Electrolux, and many others have added a design executive to the top corporate officers. Why? Because corporations have discovered that good design can be very profitable; they have found that in a world where products quickly become commodities, design helps to create a protected competitive space. But without support at a senior level, design is often overlooked in the product development process.

Designers understand that good design is good business, but quite frankly, many analytical thinkers don't really get it. So companies are adding designers to product teams and are training the more analytical team members to think like designers as well. In the software-intensive product space it would be wise to pay attention to this trend, because a large percentage of software products are focused on delivering exceptional experiences. And exceptional experiences do not happen by accident; they come from a product team with a deep understanding of design.

Case: Sphere of Influence

Sphere of Influence is a successful firm in the Washington, DC, area, serving both government and commercial customers. The company calls itself a "software product studio," which is not the same as being a conventional software company or an industrial design studio, but it has a lot in common with both. For the past 12 years, Sphere of Influence's studio of about 50 creative and technical people has been integrating design agency creative workflows with large-scale software development, allowing the company to build a considerable contracting practice.

The story of how the firm evolved from agile development to product-level design is best told by its managing partner, Theresa Smith.

From Agile to Design

—Written by Theresa Smith, Sphere of Influence

This journey began where many agile software developers start: a demanding customer, a statement of objectives, and an impossible schedule. Of course, agile seemed a perfect fit and we jumped in hook, line, and sinker. Success was an on-time delivery of high-quality code with lots of features valued by the people requesting the software. The client was deeply involved and integral to every detail of the process, providing daily prioritization, guidance, and feedback to the product team.

The software was successfully delivered, chock-full of high-priority features that had been deemed important by the client—all within a nearly impossible schedule. The final software was good and our client expressed their satisfaction with our work.

Just One Problem: The Client Was Only Satisfied

This was just one example of many where the trend was becoming clear. Our agile projects were consistently producing affordable, high-quality software with almost every customer priority included. From this perspective agile delivered elevated performance. However, when evaluating the product, not the project, an honest critic would admit these products lacked greatness. Stakeholders might have been satisfied with project performance, but rarely was the audience delighted, wowed, or blown away by novel innovation or creative design. Agile's intense focus on customer priorities amplified by the grind of just-in-time iteration created a substantial headwind against any effort to design engaging experiences, wholeness, likability, or even innovation into products. Software emerged as if it was thought about one customer-driven feature at a time and then implemented, which is not far from what happened.

It became evident that conventional agile (i.e., agile/Scrum) lacked the creative workflows to discover the right product to build. Agile also gave no guidance on how to manipulate feature mix, form, context, dominance, or cognitive engagement to impute a stronger meaning in a software product.

Strong Centers

We began using the term *Strong Center* to express the aspect of a product's identity and virtue that emerges from its wholeness. We realized the hard part wasn't executing within cost, schedule, and feature boundaries; the hard part was to use those boundaries to do something excellent. As we discovered, this required a more disciplined creative innovation process than anything available in agile literature. Agile depends on the Product Owner and other stakeholders having clairvoyance to guide a project toward a coherent, unified, and inventive product. Unfortunately, clairvoyance is insufficient as an innovation strategy. It comes down to a question of where the vision for the product originates and how that vision is manifested in thousands of decisions that together cause a Strong Center to emerge.

Having turned our attention from the project to the product, we could see our products for what they really were: average and bland. We did not want our clients to be "satisfied"; we wanted them to be "thrilled and delighted." Thus, we set out to make changes. First, we acknowledged that a development studio has an obligation to make a great product. We realized our job isn't to defer design to the client and simply transform user stories and requirements into correct programming syntax; we have a responsibility to invent technology and design engaging software by making decisions that clients and their users would never make. Second, we budgeted time for product conceptual design as a distinct activity, not something that would be performed simultaneously within agile sprints. Third, we embraced the fact that trusted agile practices were insufficient for innovation and product design and in some situations could actually interfere with those activities.

Small Beginnings

We didn't know where to start since our clients were accustomed to having 100% control over scope. On our first try we aimed small by going "under the radar," asserting our design influence over just a few pieces of a product already under development. We selected sections of the product we thought could make a difference if they were done properly yet were likely to receive little or no attention under customer-driven prioritization. These sections of the product were beneath the stakeholder attention floor; stakeholder concentration was fixated on higher-level business workflows and other important things. At this point we had yet to adopt the term *product design* for what we were doing, but we instinctively knew this was lacking and thus directed our attention there. Unlike our clients, who don't know much about software because it's not their core businesses, software is all we know and thus our opinions about user interaction and algorithm-driven automation are much more refined than the clients'. Instead of deferring to the client to make poorly informed decisions about these things, we applied our own expertise to a few confined corners of the product.

After the product successfully launched, we went back to the client with a satisfaction survey and discovered that, same as before, they were "satisfied" with the product as a whole. However, they were not satisfied with those pieces we did on our own; they were delighted! They described the overall product as "satisfactory" and more or less consistent with expectations, but they described those parts we did on our own as fantastic, saying they "made the product." We were never sure if the client even realized that we went off the reservation, but they liked what they got and that's what mattered. This gave us the confidence we needed to expand on what we were doing.

Over the next couple of projects the idea was not to pursue innovations that would change the world, but to spend a little dedicated time and energy discovering better ways to interact with users and support the client's business through a more refined product. Increasingly we directed our attentions to the Product over the Project.

There were no established agile practices suitable to guide or inspire us. Instead we looked toward industries known for their creativity and innovation—namely, industrial design and marketing studios. We spent a lot of time researching companies like IDEO, Frog, Crispin Porter + Bogusky, and others. We discovered a vast universe of ideas and techniques for executing the front end of innovation and making products better through design. Our minds were opened to the science of ethnography and how it can be applied to product development. We taught ourselves the psychology of audience engagement and discovered myriad techniques for manipulating engagement intensity. None of this is found in software development books, yet we found that it exists in a relatively mature form once we looked in the right places.

With paying clients clamoring for features and ship dates it was tempting to simply focus on implementation and delivery, but we forced ourselves to devote significant time and energy to product design and product innovation.

Making Things That Resonate

As we became more sophisticated about design, we started honing our philosophy. We completely embraced the Gestalt view that a great product is more than a concentration of high-priority features; a great product has a unified wholeness that makes use of similarity, continuation, closures, proximity, figure, and ground. We developed the belief that every feature and design element participates in groups of "unified wholes," aka "centers," that ultimately force the emergence of identity and meaningfulness. This emergent quality of design was best described by Christopher

Alexander (civil architect), first in his book *The Synthesis of Form* and later in his four-volume series *The Nature of Order*. We adopted Alexander's view that Strong Centers emerge from wholeness. We believe, as he does, that products lacking a Strong Center will fail to resonate with audiences but products with Strong Centers generally delight audiences.

This Gestalt philosophy helped us understand more clearly the purpose of a software company. It isn't to facilitate the prioritization of features and user stories, then implement them. We discovered that our purpose is to create great products with Strong Centers. We learned to impose new constraints on our work; for example, a feature belongs in a product only if it helps a Strong Center emerge. We no longer allowed features if they inhibited the formation of a Strong Center because such features interfere with the audience having a positive response to the product, even when there is high demand for the features. We found ways to fulfill unserved needs without cluttering the product.

Learning to design products so they have Strong Centers was only the first challenge. As software developers we also needed to learn how to make interactive experiences resonate. We were already well aware of usability engineering but considered the resulting products bland. We realized interaction design isn't just about usability (counting mouse clicks and tracking eye fixations); it is about creating meaning and engaging people in complex layered activities so they lose track of time and forget everything outside the experience. To learn how to do this we sought inspiration from experts in engagement psychology, not usability or user interface design. By studying people like Nancy Duarte (public speaking) and Margaret Robertson (video games), we learned that designers use cadence to engage audiences and overcome blandness. The word *resonate* itself implies that the natural vibration ("vibe") of a product is on the same frequency as the audience. It turns out there are optimal transitions and timings that, like the golden ratio, seem to resonate with people at a base level. By varying the intensity of user engagement according to these timings and transitions, we learned to entice users into what behavioral psychologist Mihaly Csikszentmihalyi calls a "flow experience." We also dove deep into a study of Gamification and developed an appreciation for subtle ways of engaging users, forcing effective learning, recognizing achievement, and acknowledging failure without making the experience depleting.

Escaping Conventionality

In most creative industries the client hires an agency because the agency has demonstrated an idea or style that resonates with the client. The understanding between client and agency acknowledges that the client is the customer and the customer is always right, but it also acknowledges that the agency is involved because it brings creativity, innovation, and a distinctive style to the product. This is the way most creative industries work, except for purpose-built software. In our industry the clients are distrustful and have been conditioned to hold vendors accountable to producing exactly what was contracted, no more and no less. There are no agencies per se, just suppliers of labor. Call it waterfall, agile, or anything else, but project management has become the center of attention, not the product. Most software development companies market their project management skills and capability maturity, not their design style or anything related to what they actually make.

Even today, our most difficult challenge is finding clients who place more value on the product than on the project management. Most prefer to initiate a relationship with an RFQ/RFP rather than ask us to pitch an innovative product concept. From our side, responding to an RFP is easy compared to pitching an innovative concept. To pitch a concept we must work through product strategy, ethnography, positioning, and conceptual design just to show up. To win we need something unique that scratches an itch the clients never knew they had while at the same time satisfying their immutable needs and objectives. The amount of work, creativity, and innovation that goes into a concept is far greater than what goes into an RFP response, not to mention the value to the client. It boggles the mind why more clients don't demand concept pitches as a selection method, but convention dictates that clients tell vendors what they want and then vendors respond with unrealistic price quotes.

Product over Project

Harvard professor Peter Rowe introduced the term **design thinking** but IDEO's David Kelley popularized the term, bringing it to the forefront—not just of industrial design but of the entire creative sector. The belief is that designers think differently and maybe even see the world differently. For example, an engineer is supposed to solve a problem by finding a minimal yet sufficient solution, whereas a designer is supposed to solve a problem by making something that is well adapted for human use. This is a distinction with a big difference. Engineers make things work, they make things efficient, and they make the process of making them efficient, regardless of whether people like or hate the thing itself. Designers exist to make things people like, often by inefficiently integrating elements and materials when doing so improves the product's overall fit for human use and perception. In all honesty, we were attracted to both engineering and design. We have the soul of engineers but the heart of designers.

We started out calling what we were doing "design thinking" but eventually abandoned that terminology. We witnessed too many examples of design for design's sake, where aesthetics trumped practicality, and where Strong Centers gave way to edginess or trendiness. While we like aesthetics and edginess, we also know that a simple old-school application can be great. We think great design is about crafting a product that imputes its virtue through Strong Centers. We are also hard-core software engineers who find elegance and beauty in things that are engineered, not just assembled. In pondering this we realized that we aren't "design people" or "engineering people"; we are actually "product people." From strategy and positioning up through design and production, the whole product is what interests us.

Sadly, we aren't in an industry where the choice is between being a "design person" and being a "product person"; in our industry everything is focused on the project, not the product. Phase-gate, waterfall, agile, and other methods all focus people's attention on the project with no guidance about what constitutes a great product.

The biggest revelation for us was realizing that our purpose is the product. Makers are remembered for the things they make, not the way they made them. This isn't a get-out-of-jail-free card when it comes to project management; it's just an adjustment of priorities. In the same way agile values People over Process, where *over* is the operative term, we say Product over Project.

Wrap It

This journey taught us that a great product has an identifiable virtue that is evident from exposure to any part of it. Every element exists and is organized expressly to reinforce the perception of the whole. The perception generally relates to what people want to get out of the product, whether an experience or an objective that may be unachievable without it.

The way our team approaches software product design requires a product designer who is able and willing to generate multiple proofs, experience them, and then assess whether a proof strengthens or weakens the identity and wholeness of the product. Every design decision is evaluated based on how it affects the strength of the perception.

When a design choice lessens the effect of the emergent properties, it lessens the strength of the Center. When the Center is weakened by a decision or element, that decision or element must be reconsidered or eliminated.

These days when we ask customers to rate our work, we find that they are not just satisfied; they *love* our products.

We asked Thad Scheer, President of Sphere of Influence, what it takes for analytical thinkers to appreciate the value of design, and what it feels like when you get there. He said:

> Design is something you can't learn by studying, practice is essential. Practice is not just essential for mastery, it's essential for understanding. Only through purposeful practice can people gain the vision to see Design and ultimately wield its power. It takes about 500 hours of practice before a person's eyes are truly opened to the world of Design. Even though Design is all around us, it's invisible (they say good Design is invisible whereas bad Design tends to be pretty apparent). It's also said that once you've had your eyes opened to the universe of Design you will never again look at a door handle the same way. It's true! This is why we capitalize the "D." While it only takes about 500 hours of dedicated practice to see Design, it takes about 2,500 hours of purposeful practice to develop any degree of proficiency with it. As with most things, it takes about 10,000 hours of purposeful practice to be good enough to compete globally. Practice is everything![11]

 Anna: It's hard to understand how customers can be convinced not to insist on their favorite features just by telling them those features aren't compatible with a "Strong Center."
M&T: Most customers appreciate good design when they see it. When customers love an experience, when they find it really engaging, they can usually be convinced to trust the people who designed that experience to know what a good product design is and what is best left out.

Otto: How do people design great products that customers love?
M&T: We think the most important lesson—and the hardest one—is to stop worrying mostly about

---

11. From private e-mail from Thad Scheer, President, Sphere of Influence. Used with permission.

technology. Stop worrying so much about getting a list of stuff done. Start spending some time visiting your customers and watching—really watching carefully—as they use your products. Every product delivers an experience, and if you don't understand the experience that your product creates, you don't really understand your product at all.

Case: A Traumatic Experience

Doug Dietz, a principal designer at GE Healthcare, had been designing MRI and CT scanners for 20 years.[12] He was immensely proud of his most recent MRI scanner design, so he went to a local hospital that had just installed this new scanner to take a look at his "baby." While he was admiring the results of the last several years of his work, a technologist asked him to step outside for a while since a patient was coming in. As he waited in the hall, he saw a girl of about seven walking down the hall with her parents. She was crying, and as she turned into the MRI room, she froze in terror.

Dietz looked at his product through the eyes of that child, and he realized that it was a failure. It was a scary, noisy, colorless contraption to a child. He found out that close to 80% of children three to seven years old have to be sedated for MRI and CT scans. He learned that a major anxiety of parents is not knowing how to help their children through the traumatic experience. He decided he was not done designing the MRI scanner until children would confidently walk into a scanning room, cooperate with technicians, and later tell their parents and friends that they enjoyed the experience.

Dietz convened a design team to achieve this goal. They started out by learning about children. They observed children at a local children's museum and talked to experts in child psychology. They got down on their hands and knees and looked at hospital scanners from a child's perspective. They listened to the noises the scanners made. They began to realize that if they could leverage the active imagination of children, they could make scanning an adventure.

 With paint, decals, and soft music they turned MRI rooms into a jungle, a spaceship, an aquarium, a campground, or a pirate ship. Children were told the story of

---

12. From Doug Dietz, "Transforming Healthcare for Children and Their Families," TEDxSanJoseCA 2012; see www.youtube.com/watch?v=jajduxPD6H4.

their MRI by their parents: *At the hospital, you will go into a magical land and climb onto a deck (or into a tent). When you get there, you must lie very still, and when you do, fish will swim over you (or monkeys will appear).*

The results were impressive. Parents were eager to get into the act, and as they relaxed, the children relaxed also. Almost no children required sedation anymore. The scans went more quickly and were of higher quality, so the MRI facility could handle more patients. Families began to ask for scans at the hospitals with child-friendly experiences. GE had new and highly recommended accessories to add to its product line. But best of all, children enjoyed their hospital experience; in fact, sometimes they asked if they could go back and do it again.

It was only because Dietz went to a children's hospital to admire an early installation of "his" MRI scanner that he realized he had missed an entire dimension of the hospital experience. Being a designer, he realized immediately that his design had a serious flaw because the experience of a very important group of consumers was traumatic. He knew the product was not finished until he found a solution to this flaw.

Designers Make Things People Like

How do designers work?

- Designers start by immersing themselves in the experience of the people who will interact with their designs. They spend a lot of time watching people. If they are designing a shopping cart, they watch people shopping.[13] If they are designing a potato peeler, they watch people peeling potatoes.[14] If they are designing a system for people to track their finances, they go to homes and watch how real people deal with finances.[15]

- Designers are not alone when they immerse themselves in the experience of consumers. People from development, quality, technical writing, marketing, production or operations, even finance, are also involved. People with different backgrounds

---

13. ABC *Nightline* produced a video of IDEO designing a shopping cart. Watch it at www.youtube.com/watch?v=M66ZU2PCIcM.

14. OXO, maker of innovative and easy-to-use kitchen tools, was founded by Sam Farber after he noticed his wife struggling to use a potato peeler.

15. Intuit's "Follow Me Home" program has a product team go home with people who have purchased its financial software and observe them as they start using the software.

bring different perspectives to the product team, and a broader perspective leads to a deeper understanding of the essential problems to be addressed.

- Designers do not take a single approach to the issues they uncover. Numerous concepts are sketched or quickly prototyped so everyone has a way to visualize the ideas. This is especially important because designers are not designing in a vacuum; they are discovering what other team members with different perspectives are thinking so as to enrich their search for an understanding of the multiple factors influencing the experience they are creating.

- Designers understand psychology; they study how people react in various situations to different stimuli. They do not accept the status quo. They ask questions, challenge assumptions, try to gain a broad view of the situation they are dealing with. Designers seek constant feedback as they develop their ideas. They change their minds and try new things. They don't consider unexpected results to be a failure; they think of surprises as a learning experience.

If you want truly delighted customers, take a page from the book of leaders of major companies who have discovered that design really matters. Help members of product teams learn to work like designers. Do not spoon-feed requirements or user stories to product teams. Ask team members to put themselves in the shoes of the people who will use their product. Expect team members to be skeptical, to ask difficult questions, and to challenge underlying assumptions, to go down multiple paths. Welcome failed experiments; worry about a failure to experiment. Above all, be sure product teams assume the responsibility for identifying and solving the right problems and thus developing the right products.

Develop the Right Products

 In Chapter 2 we discussed cognitive biases and various strategies to counteract their influence. By now you may have noticed that design is a good antidote for cognitive biases. Designers take time to observe carefully, question assumptions, and explore many possibilities—all good strategies for combating decision-making flaws such as confirmation bias. But as useful as design approaches are, many companies fail to use them when creating product road maps. It is rare that strategic planning includes planning to learn about the merits of various choices. Leadership teams tend to limit their strategic choices to whether or not to proceed (one option), or at best to either/or decisions (two options).

This approach is similar to that of the glider pilots who preceded the Wright brothers; strategic planners put together the equivalent of a glider and hope that it will fly. It is a rare leadership team that pursues the equivalent of building a wind tunnel, that asks itself the critical question *What product strategy options are available and how can we intelligently decide which option will give the best results?*

Case: Procter & Gamble

When A. G. Lafley took over as CEO of Procter & Gamble (P&G) in 2000, the company was in trouble. It was missing its financial targets and its stock price was falling precipitously. And no wonder—P&G had developed only one successful new brand in the last 15 years, and the other brands were looking rather old. When Lafley retired eight years later, revenue had more than doubled and earnings had more than quadrupled. Old brands were revived or sold off and new ones were launched. Lafley had turned P&G into one of the most innovative companies in the world.

How did he do it? Lafley focused relentlessly on innovation, launching many successful initiatives, such as the "Connect and Develop" program aimed at finding innovative ideas outside of the company and developing them into P&G products.

One of Lafley's more successful initiatives was to increase the company's focus on consumers and the design of the consumer experience. He tapped Claudia Kotchka to be Vice President of Design Innovation and Strategy and asked her to bring design thinking to the company. She hired designers and supported them when they refused to give up their Macs or work in cubicles; she found them group spaces where they could brainstorm and test ideas together. She sent a product team to a design session at IDEO and got a call from a panicked manager about their chaotic design process. "Give them a chance," Kotchka urged, and by the end of the week, the "aha" moment finally came. She tirelessly expanded her efforts to instill a company-wide focus on the customer experience as a whole.

Scientific Planning

 But perhaps Lafley's most interesting initiative was bringing the scientific method to strategic planning.[16] It was obvious that traditional planning was not working; otherwise how could the company be in such big trouble? So Lafley decided to require scientific planning—planning in which several hypotheses are framed and tested—rather than planning in which a single course of action is chosen and executed. The new approach would require that managers stop asking, *What should we do?* and start asking, *What might we do?* This is a different way of thinking for many managers, especially those who take pride in being "decisive."

Lafley insisted that planning teams frame a minimum of two mutually exclusive courses of action to resolve any key business issue. More options were better. One option was not acceptable; it would amplify any tendency toward confirmation bias. Therefore, the scientific planning process started by generating a long and unfiltered list of strategic possibilities. Of course, people on the leadership team would be deeply skeptical of many of these possibilities, so the next step was for the skeptics to state what conditions had to be true in order for them to believe that a possibility would work. In other words, managers had to shift from asking, *What do I believe about this possibility?* to asking, *What would I have to believe in order to support this possibility?* In order to answer the second question, managers had to imagine that ideas that they did not like could actually be great ideas—which was no easy task.

A leadership team could not start evaluating the possibilities until they understood the conditions necessary to make each possibility successful. Only then could they discuss which of the conditions needed for the success of a possibility were the least likely to hold true. Skeptics were important for this step, because they were the most likely to understand the biggest barriers to success.

Lafley suggested that the person who was most skeptical be asked to design a test to prove whether the barrier she or he saw was actually real. The entire team had to agree that the test was valid and proper judgments could be formed on whether or not to proceed based on the test results. Tests had to be detailed and focused on a single barrier to

---

16. Information in this section is from A. G. Lafley, Roger L. Martin, Jan W. Rivkin, and Nicolaj Siggelkow, "Bringing Science to the Art of Strategy," *Harvard Business Review*, September 2012.

success. The biggest barrier was investigated first, because if it failed, no further investigation was needed, making the testing process relatively efficient. In those cases where the first test passed, less critical barriers were tested, one at a time, until the team was convinced that the possibility could succeed.

To summarize the P&G approach to scientific planning:[17]

1. **Frame a choice.** Convert each business issue into at least two mutually exclusive options that might resolve it.

2. **Generate possibilities.** Broaden the list of options to ensure an inclusive range of possibilities.

3. **Specify conditions.** For each possibility, describe what must be true for it to be sound.

4. **Identify barriers.** Determine which conditions are least likely to hold true.

5. **Design tests.** For each key barrier condition, devise a test the team agrees is valid and sufficient to generate commitment.

6. **Conduct the tests.** Start with the tests for the barrier conditions in which there is the least confidence.

7. **Make a choice.** Review the key conditions in light of the test results in order to reach a decision.

The best part about scientific planning is that it combats cognitive biases through careful experimentation around a broad array of possibilities. Product teams learn to ask challenging questions—questions that designers would find familiar:

1. What are the possibilities?

2. What has to be true in order for a possibility to succeed?

3. What experiments can we run to see if those things are true?

> **Anna:** I like the idea of using the scientific method to develop strategy. I like decisions that are based on data.
> **M&T:** We like the fact that a scientific process tends to keep people from jumping to conclusions. We also like the idea that skeptics are forced to play devil's advocate against their own skepticism.

---

17. Ibid.

A Design Toolbox

As Theresa Smith noted earlier in this chapter, there are many well-known tools and techniques that designers use to help them create engaging experiences. We will list a few here along with references for those who wish to explore these tools further.

Establish Empathy

The first step in creating the right product is to help the product team establish empathy with their audience. There are many approaches to developing empathy; among our favorites are journey mapping and adoption chain analysis.

> Journey map:[18] A journey map is a visualization of the experience of potential customers as they struggle trying to do some job—a job that will be improved by the new product. A journey map is similar to a value stream map, only it is a map of the *customer's* value stream, not the product team's value stream. The goal of a journey map is to help members of the product team understand how their potential customers currently do a job and discover opportunities for improvement.
>
> To create a journey map, product team members develop a deep understanding of target customers' experiences through observation and interviews or, better yet, by doing the job themselves. During and after the fieldwork, team members capture what they observe with sketches, photographs, video clips, or any other technique that conveys the essence of what they observed. It is important to capture emotions; the frustrations and challenges of doing the job are one of the most fruitful areas for introducing innovation.
>
> After product team members experience the problems and frustrations of the job they will be improving, they work together to draw a map of the customer's journey, complete with the idiosyncrasies and roadblocks that make the job difficult. This forms the basis for identifying the biggest opportunities for improvement and thus the most important features of the new product.

---

18. See Jeanne Liedtka and Tim Ogilvie, *Designing for Growth* (Columbia University Press, 2011).

Adoption chain analysis:[19] Many organizations are usually involved in making a complex product successful. Inside a company there are various stakeholders whose cooperation is essential. In a marketplace, there are complementors whose involvement is required for success. For example, a mobile application must work on a mobile platform, may acquire data from a third party, may be sold through a partner, and could run entirely in the cloud.

Each of those complementors must do its part in order for the application to work, and they will cooperate only if they see a benefit in doing so. If the third party sees no benefit in supplying the data, or target customers cannot readily access the cloud service, the new product will fail.

Mapping out the benefits of each party in the adoption chain helps the product team imagine the reaction of all involved parties. What the team is looking for is any party in the adoption chain that might not see the benefit in doing its part, because if they don't cooperate, the product will not be successful. If a complementor is found that has little incentive to cooperate, the product team has discovered a critical adoption problem that must be addressed.

Generate Possibilities

Generating multiple possibilities is essential to designing great products, especially when product development is going to be expensive. It is better to examine the options in the planning stage than to discover them after it's too late to change course. There are several tools for considering possibilities, including sample press releases and impact maps.

Press release:[20] At Amazon.com, teams are expected to *work backward* from customers to define the minimum product capability needed to accomplish their objective. To do this, they often write a sample press release aimed at the people who would use the product. The press release defines what the product will do to make a customer's life easier, why the customer will love it, and how to get started.

---

19. See Ron Adner, *The Wide Lens: A New Strategy for Innovation* (Penguin Publishing, 2012), especially Chapter 3, "Adoption Chain Risk: Seeing All the Customers before Your End Customer."
20. See www.allthingsdistributed.com/2006/11/working_backwards.html.

A press release is similar to a project charter, but it starts with customers in mind rather than stakeholder priorities. If the product team has difficulty writing a press release, the members probably do not have a clear vision of the essential features of the product.

Impact map:[21] An impact map is a visual planning technique by which a product team clarifies the following issues about the product they will develop:

- **Goals:** *Why* are we creating this product? What measurable goals are we expecting to achieve?
- **Actors:** *Who* can significantly impact the success of the product? Who will use it? Who will be significantly affected by the product?
- **Impacts:** *How* will the actors be involved in achieving the goals? What do they have to do? How should our product change their behavior?
- **Deliverables:** *What* choices do we have in designing the product? What tests will demonstrate which choices provide the greatest impact?
- **Assumptions:** *What* assumptions are exposed by the impact map? How can we test these assumptions?

Run Experiments

Running market tests prior to full-scale development is a time-honored approach to product development. But small-scale experiments can be run long before a product is developed and released even to a test market.[22]

Assumption testing: An important tool for finding the right problem is to expose and then examine the assumptions behind various possibilities. At P&G, planners learn to generate many possibilities and then for each possibility ask, *What would have to be true in order for this possibility to work?*

---

21. See Gojko Adzic, *Impact Mapping* (Provoking Thoughts, 2012).
22. These three well-known tools are discussed in detail in Liedtka and Ogilvie, *Designing for Growth*.

Rapid prototyping: Prototypes should be built early and often. Prototypes convey ideas, allow many mistakes to be made and discarded quickly, and are absolutely necessary for really solid ideas to emerge. Early ideas are just steps on the road to better ideas. Designers would never present only one idea to a client.

Learning launch: In the software world it can be easy to deliver new software to production every day, measure actual customer reactions, then adapt based on what was learned. This is similar to the Lean Startup approach, which we will discuss further in Chapter 4.

Questions to Ponder

1. What does the word *design* mean to you? Does it mean figuring out how to structure software? Or does it mean making something that people love?

2. Can you reduce the product you are currently working on to a few essential (wicked) problems to be solved—the way Wilbur Wright reduced flying to three essential systems?

3. If you surveyed your customers, would they be delighted with your work? Or would they be "just" satisfied? What would have to change in order to have most of your customers *love* your work?

4. Have you ever pitched a product concept to a customer (similar to a design agency) instead of responding to an RFP? Are there any circumstances that might prompt you to do this?

5. Starting with a blank slate (pretend everyone in development just won the lottery and left), what kind of expertise is important in designing the products your organization develops?

6. Imagine that you are looking at an early installation of a product you recently finished, and you see a serious problem with the customer experience, the same way Doug Dietz saw a young child terrified of his MRI scanner. Would you redesign the product to fix the problem? Would your company support the redesign?

7. How many possibilities does your organization usually generate before product development begins? How are these possibilities investigated?

8. Is decisiveness considered an important trait in your company? Why or why not? What is the value of decisiveness?

9. Can you write a press release for the product or project that you are currently working on? Would potential customers be eager to try the product based on that press release?

10. What other parties will have to contribute something or do something in order for your product to be a success? What motivation do they have to help you out?

4

Genuine Efficiency

What Is Efficiency?

The most efficient retail stores—the stores that can afford to offer customers the lowest prices and best values—are the stores that pay the highest wages, offer the best benefits, and provide stable, full-time employment.[1]

The most efficient U.S. airline—the one that has the lowest labor costs per passenger mile—is the one that pays employees the highest salaries and has never had an involuntary layoff.[2]

The most efficient customer service centers—the ones that have the fewest calls and the most satisfied customers—do *not* focus on worker productivity; they focus on understanding the causes behind customer calls and on eliminating those causes.[3]

The most efficient product development organizations—the ones that design the most valuable products—are not the ones that deliver the most features, but the ones that deliver only the right features.[4]

---

1. See Chapter 1 for further discussion and also Ton, "Why 'Good Jobs' Are Good for Retailers."
2. See Jeffrey Pfeffer, "Lay Off the Layoffs," *Newsweek*, February 5, 2010; and Greg J. Bamber, Jody Hoffer Gittell, Thomas A. Kochan, and Andrew von Nordenflycht, "Up in the Air: How Airlines Can Improve Performance by Engaging Their Employees," *Newsweek*, February 5, 2010, especially pp. 87–96.
3. John Seddon, *Freedom from Command and Control: Rethinking Management for Lean Service* (Productivity Press, 2005).
4. See Stefan Thomke and Donald Reinertsen, "Six Myths of Product Development," *Harvard Business Review*, May 2012.

Product development efficiency is not about skimping on product development costs; it is about focusing creative minds on the job of developing successful products. The only viable measure of development efficiency is the ratio of effort expended to overall product performance.

In their excellent book *This Is Lean: Resolving the Efficiency Paradox*,[5] Niklas Modig and Par Ahlstrom distinguish between resource efficiency (keeping everyone busy) and flow efficiency (keeping the work flowing). They show how an intense focus on resource efficiency introduces intractable wastes such as queues, handovers, and thrashing. Truly efficient organizations focus primarily on flow efficiency, which provides a holistic view of the system and inevitably produces better overall results.

 Anna: Some people think efficiency means being "lean and mean"—which often means layoffs, low salaries, outsourced development, and call center scripts. Are you saying those practices are not efficient?

M&T: Right. Those practices are not lean nor are they efficient. A company with a lean mindset leverages the intelligence of its people and does not tolerate insensitive treatment of workers. Why not? Because the evidence clearly shows that practices that demoralize workers make it impossible to have genuine, sustainable efficiency. Lean leaders understand that true efficiency comes from flow, from speed, from learning, and from workers who care.

Lessons in Flow: Ericsson

Ericsson is a leading supplier of telecommunications infrastructure—all the stuff behind phones that ties them together and makes them smart. The company was founded in Sweden in 1876 and has thrived for well over a century in the dynamic telecom industry. Over the past decade, the pace of change in telecommunications has accelerated, and the focus has shifted from hardware to software. So a few years ago, leaders in Ericsson Networks development units began to realize that their old—and very successful—approach to developing products was

---

5. Niklas Modig and Par Ahlstrom, *This Is Lean: Resolving the Efficiency Paradox* (Rheologica Publishing, 2012).

not going to take them much further. They needed to bring software-intensive products to market much faster and in a more predictable manner than business as usual allowed.

This section chronicles the journey of two Ericsson Networks development units from a big-batch development process to a continuous flow process. In the first development unit, change was driven by an urgent need to decrease time to market. The second unit was motivated by a keen desire for more predictable performance.

Case 1: Faster Time to Market

 When it became clear that past development practices would not deliver new product capabilities at the speed demanded by an increasingly competitive market, managers in an Ericsson Networks development unit laid out a high-level framework for implementing a substantial change in product development. They would switch from the traditional model of release-oriented projects to a lean and agile model that was centered on fast, focused feature development in empowered feature teams. The transition would be gradual, one product area at a time, and most important, the individual teams would be expected to work out the details of the new process.

The first step was to change the composition of teams. Existing teams were organized around functions; the new teams would be interdisciplinary teams of about seven people. As they were formed, teams received a brief introduction to the new approach:

- The program office will track desired features and integration dependencies for products and maintain a continually updated, prioritized list of desired features.

- Each team will choose (or be given) a feature from somewhere near the top of the priority list. The team is expected to figure out how to deliver that feature.

- Each feature will have a time constraint (on the order of weeks) determined by its value and market need; the team is expected to finish within that timebox.

- Features will be described as a high-level goal; teams are expected to decide on the details, sometimes by working with a sales engineer, to decide what scope will meet the goal within the timebox.

- Team members are expected to decide how they will work together; if they need additional expertise, they are expected to arrange for it themselves.

- Work must be continuously integrated into the common code base so as to find defects immediately, keep the code clean, and uncover hidden dependencies.

- A team should work on one feature at a time. Only when it is tested, integrated, and ready to deploy should the team move on to the next feature.

- Releases will be decoupled from features and scheduled at frequent intervals; any features that are done will be packaged into the next release.

The message was clear: "We know at a high level what customers want and when. We expect you to figure out the details of each feature and how to implement it, and we will support you."

The results were fast and dramatic. Change requests, along with all the time and energy they used to absorb, just simply disappeared. Since nothing was decided until as late as possible, no time needed to be spent changing the "plan." Internal trouble reports decreased significantly, because most issues were resolved at the source, within the interdisciplinary teams. Build time decreased dramatically; in one isolated case it went from 17 hours on a good day to a reliable five minutes. There was no rocket science behind shortening build times; it's just that when you build only once every few months, it doesn't have to be fast. But when you build several times a day to sync the work of several teams, well, you quickly invest the time in shortening the build times.

 The primary objective of the transformation was faster time to market, and sure enough, the time from start of development to field trial was cut in half. Quality also increased; there were fewer defects on the main branch and fewer defects reported from customers. In addition, more work got done; after fine tuning, hours per feature was sometimes reduced by 50+%. And they were the right features: Sales engineers reported that the feature "hit rate" increased; the product was much better at meeting the customers' expectations. This was no doubt due to the improved quality of the dialog between the development organization and customers; the time between a request from customers and the response of the development organization was much shorter, and some development teams were able to get regular feedback from customers.

Perhaps most important of all, the feedback from team members was amazing. One very senior engineer was overheard saying, "In the old days, allocation of people to multiple projects led to waste because of context switching and restarts. When the going got tough, people ran away to other projects. Now we solve the problem together." Another team leader said, "By working closely together solving the problem, nowadays we use our whole brain capacity."

Organization

In an interview with involved managers, we asked how roles changed as a result of the new organization. Probably the most challenging issue, they said, was preserving a single product while expecting multiple teams to be independently responsible for feature delivery. They addressed this by having architects and component specialists act as the "glue between teams." Architects and specialists maintained responsibility for their technical area, but they were expected to support the teams rather than assume responsibility for features. So these experts evolved from a role that involved breaking down requirements and feeding them to teams to a role of a teacher and communicator, helping teams figure out the details for themselves. This role was easier for some specialists than for others, but over time the matrix approach has turned out to be an excellent approach to scaling. It allowed Ericsson to maintain much of the existing organizational structure and the value it provided, making it a "safe" approach. At the same time, it has proven to be an effective structure for transitioning to small, responsible teams while maintaining coherence across a large product.

In the past, when teams had the need for a component specialist, they would ask for help and wait until a specialist was available. In the new system, it was made clear that this was not going to happen: "You have the people that you have, and you have to solve the problem. If you need to ask your colleague for help, go ahead and do so." Interestingly, this caused an informal system of reciprocity to develop between teams: "If you help our team out today, we'll help you out tomorrow." This system was not particularly visible to management, but it was very effective at getting things done.

Of course, while the small teams focus on delivering features, the big picture still needs attention. The program office remains responsible for product-level planning, architectural runway work, as well as "anatomy planning" (breaking up a feature that is large to be implemented step by step by one team). The program office encourages an approach called "*lagomisering*" or "just enough." The idea is to focus on critical functionality first, or "minimum marketable features." Later on, if something that was left out begins to hurt, it gets added. It turns out that it is much easier to add things later than it is to reduce the scope of premature decisions. This philosophy is implemented at two levels. At the high level, the "right features" are selected just before development starts, and at a detailed level, development teams determine the behavior of a feature "just in time."

Software development is done at two sites in this development unit, many time zones apart. The transition planners had no intention of letting this affect teams, so all members of a feature team are at a single location. When it is necessary for work to be coordinated across sites, people are expected to travel and talk to each other. On the whole, because responsibility for complete features is given to a team at a single site, distributed locations do not have much impact on the development process.

Case 2: Predictable Delivery

 Meanwhile, another Ericsson Networks development unit was looking for a more predictable development process so it could make more reliable promises to customers. The leaders began discussions with project managers, business unit managers, technology managers, designers, integration, verification, certification, and deployment people to get an end-to-end perspective on their development process. Working together, these teams "discovered" the Cone of Uncertainty:[6] "The further away from delivery we are, the more uncertainty we have."

Accepting that in product development you can't predict precisely when development will be done, the leaders decided that estimates really should be expressed as ranges: shortest time, probable time, longest time. They also realized that trying to plan ahead in large project-size chunks was a waste of time; there was too much uncertainty. Borrowing ideas from the earlier agile transformation we described in Case 1, managers decided to abandon projects, which were big batches of features, and manage development on a feature-by-feature basis instead. Releases would be divorced from feature development and

6. The Cone of Uncertainty was introduced by Barry Boehm in his 1981 book *Software Engineering Economics* (Prentice Hall). It diagrams the certainty of project estimates against time. At the beginning of a project, estimates are likely to be wrong by a factor of four; they gradually become more accurate as the project proceeds.

occur at regular intervals; whatever features were ready for release by the deadline would be included in the release.

An agile transition plan was developed that established cross-functional feature teams of about seven people. A team has a technical leader (called a Product Owner) who works closely with a Product Manager (located at headquarters). Each team works on the next most important feature, one feature at a time. Features can be quite large, so a feature often requires multiple teams. These teams are coordinated by a feature leader and through regular meetings of people on the contributing teams. Although the development organization is spread across six sites around the world, teams working on a feature are ideally located at a single site.

To implement this transformation, the leadership team focused on three things: culture, practices and processes, and organizational structure.

1. **Culture.** "Since we are living in uncertain times, let's not make it worse by hiding things," one manager said. *Teams are trusted to do their best work*, and they do, which removes the need for escalations. Weekly estimates of the completion ranges of each feature are sent to the planning group, which graphs them. The manager sketched a sample graph (Figure 4-1) and explained:

   On the top you see time, with the vertical line being the next release date. Each pending feature has a range of completion dates, submitted by the team. The shaded portion is the range of uncertainty. In this case, if these are four features we want to get into the next release, we can see that features 1 and 2 are probably OK. Feature 3 is definitely at risk and feature 4 probably needs attention. But we can see these problems long in advance so we have plenty of time to add more teams to a feature, take things out of a feature, or move the feature into the next release.

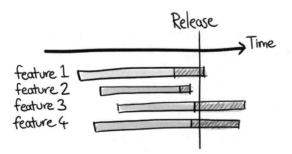

Figure 4-1
Sketch of weekly
planning graph

2. **Practices and processes.** The organization decided to use Scrum as its process and trained trainers and coaches, who then trained and coached teams. They allowed the prior projects to complete as scheduled, and over the course of a year, as projects ended, new feature teams were formed.

3. **Organizational structure.** The group also changed its organizational structure to support the feature teams. Architectural review of all features is provided on a frequent basis—usually weekly—to maintain product integrity across teams.

 The results are remarkable. After 18 months, every release has been on time and contained the desired features. Quality is significantly improved. Technical debt is being paid off. Because there is no attempt to forecast too far into the future, reliable commitments are made and kept. Teams stay together and make their own decisions on how best to do work. As one manager said, "We had to let go to gain control."

Summary

Ericsson Networks is still working through the transition process, and because there is a strong emphasis on local choice, there are many different implementations of a lean and agile approach inside the organization. Some development areas focus on implementing specific agile practices. Other areas emphasize rapid flow and short feedback loops between customers and development teams, encouraging teams to find better ways to do that. But in all cases, people are working in interdisciplinary teams, learning from each other, and focusing on customers. The net result is that many, many more intelligent, creative minds are being brought to bear on the fundamental imperative—rapid, reliable response to a very rapidly changing marketplace.

Anna: It's hard to believe that Ericsson abandoned projects.

M&T: Ericsson had been organized along functional lines, with project managers responsible for delivering product capabilities by coordinating expertise across functions. This structure had a long and successful history, but it resulted in several problems. First of all, handovers of information between functions tended to be inefficient; both knowledge and time were lost in every handover. As the number of handovers increased, the problems tended to escalate nonlinearly. Furthermore, workers in each function were assigned to multiple projects, causing severe multitasking that increased inefficiencies. The inefficiencies of handovers and multitasking showed up as decreased speed, and therefore slower time to market.

Projects often create artificial coupling between features that can, and generally should, be thought of as separate concepts. Abandoning projects was a key step in helping teams think about individual features in a more holistic, customer-focused way. Organizing around features also helps eliminate multitasking, because teams work on one feature at a time.

Finally, managing flow gives managers more control and delivers more predictable results than managing a task-based schedule, as we saw in Case 2.

Otto: It seems to me that those teams aren't really autonomous; they have central planning and a central architecture group.

M&T: Ericsson is a platform creator, and platforms are complex systems. Any company creating platforms must create a very complex infrastructure, whether it's Amazon's Web Services or Apple's App Store or Google's Search infrastructure or Facebook's Platform. With such a large, complex infrastructure, there is a need for system-level coordination and architecture.

Let's look at Case 1 in more detail. In the interest of speed, small, permanent, interdisciplinary teams were given the responsibility to deliver one feature at a time. Team members had limited control over which feature they worked on and how much time they had, but quite a bit of control over the details of the feature and how they would implement it. The features were chosen from the current most important customer concerns, so teams were working on things that really mattered.

As much as possible, decision-making authority shifted from functional specialists and project managers to small, multidiscipline teams that were trusted to make good decisions. Teams were provided with a supporting structure that designed the overall product strategy and maintained the integrity of the product's architecture and components. Teams accepted their responsibility, occasionally supplementing the formal support systems with an informal network of reciprocity in order to meet their commitments.

In the end, the product reached the market twice as fast. This does not necessarily mean that the same amount of work got done in half the time; what really happened was that the *right* work got done in half the time (the hit rate increased). Many other good things happened as well. Quality increased. Engineer engagement increased. Sales engineers were delighted. These are the kinds of results that flow-based systems are known to deliver.

Lessons in Speed: CareerBuilder[7]

Back in the day when the Internet was starting to become popular—say, the late 1990s—there were plenty of startups rushing to establish a viable business in this new territory. CareerBuilder was among them. Its small software development team used Microsoft's tools of the time: Visual Basic for the client, Active Server Pages (ASP) for the servers, COM objects for communication between the two. They built the Web site quickly and deployed software whenever something was ready. They built a path for moving available jobs from a client company's database into the CareerBuilder database, a way for people to search for jobs, and an ever-expanding number of additional capabilities.

The company was successful. It grew. It made some acquisitions. The software got complicated. A homegrown messaging layer was put between the clients and the servers to reduce dependencies. For a while this worked, and developers were still able to deploy their own software as soon as it was developed. The success, and the growth, continued. By 2003 there were around three dozen developers supporting a good number of services. The complexity began to get out of hand again, as it always does when growth increases dependencies beyond the capability of an organization to manage them.

About that time two things happened: Microsoft introduced .NET, and CareerBuilder IT leaders discovered the authors' recently published book, *Lean Software Development*. They decided to use the .NET toolset to get complexity under control and to use lean development principles to guide decisions about how to approach the transition. Following lean principles, CareerBuilder moved to .NET gradually, testing changes inside of the existing system, tackling the most difficult challenge first.

---

7. CareerBuilder.com is the largest and most visited online job site in the United States, and its technology powers more than 10,000 other career sites. CareerBuilder employs approximately 2,000 people and has a presence in over 60 markets worldwide. Information in this section is from an interview with CareerBuilder CTO Eric Presley.

With the arrival of .NET, all software had to be compiled and checked out before it was deployed, which was considered a significant advantage. On the other hand, the local, on-demand deployment that had served the company so well for so long was no longer possible. Releases had to be synchronized across all programs in the entire system. For the first time, CareerBuilder began to experience the pain of system-wide releases. Leaders began to ask themselves, *How often do we want to deal with this pain? Should we continue to release the system daily? How about weekly? Maybe monthly?*

Rejecting False Trade-offs

Everyone at CareerBuilder had grown used to the small, rapid changes that daily deployments delivered, and it was difficult to imagine giving up such responsiveness. At the time, most companies believed that speed and high quality were mutually exclusive. However, the CareerBuilder team studied lean concepts and came to the conclusion that this was a false trade-off. They understood that high speed goes hand in hand with serious discipline and excellent quality. Therefore, they decided that they did not have to give up daily deployment to get high quality; instead, they had to figure out how to add the discipline to make it work.

Releasing daily was hard and caused a lot of pain. But instead of abandoning the idea, CareerBuilder looked for ways to make it work better. Developers learned about Test Driven Development (TDD) and started using unit test frameworks. The company adopted Selenium to provide automated functional testing. As the prerelease tests became more extensive and builds became more frequent, CareerBuilder made significant investments of time and money to reduce the time this took. They invested in people, in virtualization, and in hardware so that they could, for example, rapidly import production data into the test environment.

The question arose, *When do you snapshot the code to run the tests for the daily release?* If the cutoff was too late and there was a problem with the build, the problem might not surface until after people went home. But moving the cutoff earlier meant development efforts late in the day would not reach production until the end of the next day. This issue became more complicated as acquisitions around the world meant code contributions were coming in from every time zone. Eventually the company came up with a release approach that is both simple and ingenious. CareerBuilder would do a worldwide build not once a day, but once an hour. Then at the end of the day, the Atlanta deployment team could release the last good build into production. Usually the last good build has occurred less than an hour—or perhaps two—earlier. This strategy worked so well that CareerBuilder began to do a second daily release—the first thing in the morning in Atlanta, which is the end of the day in Shanghai.

Organizing for Speed

From the earliest days, product development leaders at CareerBuilder embraced the lean mandate *Limit Work to Capacity*. They understood that an overloaded system slows everything down, and they considered speed to be fundamental to success. CareerBuilder has about 30 product areas—areas such as Job Posting, Résumé Database, Search, and so on. Each product area is allocated either one or two queues of work; each queue is handled by one or two developers (usually two). A queue may have one active project and up to three waiting projects—never more. Projects must be small—no longer than three weeks. Thus, a queue will never contain more than a quarter's worth of work for two people. A busy Career-Builder product area with two queues is depicted in Figure 4-2.

Product area queues are maintained by a business partner and supported by a team of five engineers. Each queue has two engineers who focus on moving the system forward to meet business needs. They are

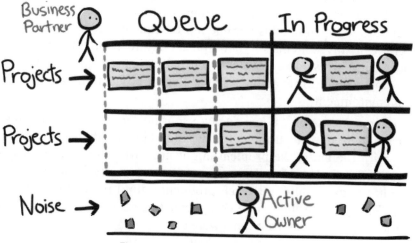

Figure 4-2   Product area team

in constant communication with their business partner to jointly decide how to solve current problems and what the product area needs next.

The product area team also includes an "Active Owner," an engineer whose job it is to deal with the noise, the dependencies with other teams, and the issues from business partners that have to be dealt with to keep the overall system healthy. The Active Owner may hold the role permanently, or developers handling the queues may rotate into the role. In either case, CareerBuilder considers the role of Active Owner to be the cost of doing business; someone has to deal with the noise generated by the complexity and dependencies of the system while teammates focus on getting projects done.

Local Responsibility

CareerBuilder has never had a quality assurance function; the development engineers are responsible for delivering high-quality products. Developers hand their work over to a central deployment group, which runs test harnesses that include both unit and functional tests. Every hour the system is built and the test harnesses are run. If the tests don't pass, it's the developer's job to find out why and fix it. This isn't too much of a burden, because after all, only an hour earlier all the tests worked, so the problem lies in the last hour's worth of work.

In the past, portfolio management was handled centrally, with the leadership team deciding which projects to put into the queues. But then the company experimented with creating dedicated teams for each product area and found that the teams, in discussion with their business partners, made good decisions on projects without much need for the centralized system. Now the management team meets weekly to monitor the projects in queues, but generally all they need to do is ensure that those projects are in line with the overall strategy.

CareerBuilder has made acquisitions around the world, with centers in Europe, India, and China. The centers are staffed to support the business in their region, because the company has found that development works best if the development teams and the business partners are in the same location or, second best, in nearby time zones. Daily deployment and short projects create a demand for close ties and frequent communication between business and technical people; there simply isn't time for information to wait a half a day to make its way across a team.

When an acquisition occurs, the new engineers learn about the benefits of the CareerBuilder platform and the development basics: daily releases, short queues, small dedicated teams that focus on business problems. And then they are urged to figure out how to get on board. Engineers from the Paris branch of CareerBuilder reported that it took about a year of hard work to get up to speed with the daily releases, but after that investment, it was difficult to imagine any other way of working.

Unlimited Learning Opportunities

CareerBuilder is a successful company competing in a very challenging and rapidly changing market. In this context, the speed and discipline imposed by daily releases have served them very well. "We feel like we have unlimited learning opportunities," says Eric Presley, CareerBuilder's CTO. "We don't have to wait to learn, and that's critically important." Developers don't have to theorize about the right approach. They can implement the simplest way they can imagine to solve a business problem—maybe taking a half day—and find out the next day if their solution is a good one. If not, customers will be very clear about what they would prefer instead. "Getting something to the users is a nonissue. It's never a discussion. You're 100% focused on the business problems at hand," Presley says.

CareerBuilder's leadership team has always valued the responsiveness that comes with daily releases, so they have never questioned the investment necessary to support an approach that many would consider unorthodox. "One of our company values is agility," Eric Presley says, "and if you're going to have agility as a company value, you'd better be releasing as fast as you can. We always understood that you're not going to see a significant benefit from lean unless the culture of the company supports it. We have always had the luxury that our company culture naturally supports lean, it supports agile as a company value, and it supports failure as it relates to learning. And we're still learning."

Eric Presley once told us he thinks the most important lean principle is *Deliver Fast*. We were surprised, but his logic was irrefutable. He explained: "If you deliver fast, you are focused on customers; you have to eliminate waste; you must have high quality; you will be constantly learning; decisions must be made at the team level; you have to keep on improving; and you are optimizing the whole system."

Otto: CareerBuilder makes daily deployment look easy.
M&T: Back in 2003, daily releases were a radical concept. Conventional wisdom at the time was that rapid deployment was extremely risky, and the tools to deal

with this risk were just being invented. It took CareerBuilder a long time to get really good at daily deployment. It certainly was not easy.

Anna: Do you think CareerBuilder made the right decision about daily deployment? It seems to have cost them a lot of money.

M&T: They absolutely made the right decision! The biggest bottleneck in most software development organizations is the huge investment in system integration at the end of a development cycle. This can easily take 30% or more of the entire cycle, and it is all waste. Instead of creating defects that are not found until days or weeks later, CareerBuilder finds defects within hours. This is a far more efficient development process. Although there was a steep learning curve in getting daily deployment working, in the end it saved CareerBuilder a lot more than it cost.

The 2010 book *Continuous Delivery*[8] by Jez Humble and Dave Farley is an authoritative and detailed summary of how to tackle the problems of frequent releases that has guided many organizations around the world. These days when we meet teams developing cloud or mobile software, or delivering software as a service, we find that most of them are trying to follow the Continuous Delivery playbook and move toward weekly, daily, or even more frequent releases.

Lessons in Learning: Lean Startup

When a company is just starting up, it is not yet worried about how often to release a product; instead, the founders ask themselves, *When should we launch our great new product the first time?* In the 1990s, product launch was a big deal, and founders wanted to be sure everything was ready and stacked for success before they took the leap. Typically that meant the product was "complete" and "ready for prime time."

One of the more pervasive mental models at the time was that "real" companies do not release products until they are "finished." This might have made a lot of sense when a product was something manufactured in a factory. But for software products, ideas about the "right" time to release software were formed back in the day when computers

---

8. Jez Humble and Dave Farley, *Continuous Delivery* (Addison-Wesley, 2010).

were big and expensive and most software developers worked in the IT departments of large companies. Software was thought to be very difficult to change, so it had to be "done" before it was released.

In fact, before the Internet, it *was* difficult to change software products. PC software was expensive to modify once the floppy disks or CDs were distributed. Even as the Internet spun up, upgrading software carried a significant overhead. But eventually, antivirus and operating system companies figured out how to push software updates to clients with very low overhead. Still, the mental model that required software products to be finished before they were launched was pervasive. Google was considered an anomaly when it started launching products in a "beta" state.

Even today, many companies assume that launching an incomplete software product is equivalent to launching a low-quality product; they fear that customers will get a bad first impression, and they worry that competitors might steal their ideas. Let's be honest; some of these concerns are justified. But not the first one, the concern for poor quality; there is no excuse for any software to have defects. As we saw at CareerBuilder, software can be constructed so as to be high quality at all times during development; any code that leaves a developer's workstation can be (and should be) free of defects.

On the other hand, worry that customers might get a bad impression from an incomplete product is a valid concern. In fact, when the product's main selling point is the experience it delivers, companies are well advised to delay launch until they get the experience right.

Finally, fear that competitors might steal an idea might be justified if the product is easy to clone. But well-designed products combined with successful business models have proven to be surprisingly difficult to copy, because there is so much more to success than meets the eye. Consider Dropbox, for example. When it was founded, there were dozens of companies selling Internet storage systems. But Dropbox had a different business model; it focused on synchronizing data (state) across multiple devices. It turns out that having the same state on multiple personal devices is increasingly convenient as devices proliferate. The important thing is no longer the device; it is the state maintained by Dropbox. It helps that Dropbox is intuitive, works on every device, and is marketed through recommendations. But it has been difficult to copy because the underlying value it delivers—device independence—had not been obvious to early competitors.

Build-Measure-Learn

 In 2011, Eric Ries published *The Lean Startup*,[9] in which he recommends using the scientific method to improve the success of startups. In the introduction he says, "Throughout my career, I kept having the experience of working incredibly hard on products that ultimately failed in the marketplace." He cites as an example the many months of intense effort that went into what he thought was a critical feature for IMVU, a company he cofounded. After the feature was launched, however, no one used it. Investigation showed that one of the basic assumptions behind the feature was dead wrong. So the months of work spent on the feature turned out to be completely wasted effort.[10]

Through experiences like this, Ries came to realize that startup companies are founded on a set of assumptions, and it's almost certain that some of those assumptions are wrong. So it is a good idea to validate the assumptions earlier rather than later. How do you do that? You don't wait until the product is completely finished before launching it; you launch a **minimum viable product** (MVP) as soon as possible and use it to test and refine assumptions. Ries notes that the only real progress made during IMVU's early months was learning about what created value for customers. Everything else they spent time on ended up being waste.[11]

The Lean Startup approach is based on the idea that the job of a startup is to learn how to build a sustainable business. The best way to do this is to validate business assumptions by running experiments that reveal the cause-and-effect relationship between product capabilities and the business results they generate. Product development becomes a series of **Build-Measure-Learn** cycles: Build a feature, measure whether it delivers the expected outcomes, learn from the results.

To illustrate this idea, Ries tells the story of Grockit, a company that had launched an acclaimed Web site to help people study together for university admission tests.[12] The development team used a highly

---

9. Eric Ries, *The Lean Startup: How Today's Entrepreneurs Use Continuous Innovation to Create Radically Successful Businesses* (Crown Business, 2011).
10. Unfortunately this is not an isolated incident; it is a very common occurrence.
11. Ries, *The Lean Startup*.
12. Ibid., pp. 129–42.

disciplined agile process and reliably delivered the features that founder Farbood Nivi (Farb) believed were most important.

But one day Ries asked development team members a simple question: "How do you know that the prioritization decisions Farb is making actually make sense?" They answered: "That is not our department. Farb makes the decisions; we execute them."[13] Think about that answer. It tells you that the Grockit development team was doing what it was asked to do, but its members did not accept responsibility for the success of the product they were developing. They left all product decisions to Farb, who had neither the time nor the tools to be sure the decisions he made were the right decisions. This is a good way for technical people to end up wasting a lot of their time working on things that don't matter in the end.

Once he understood the power of the Build-Measure-Learn cycle, Farb asked the development team to become engaged in the entire cycle and share responsibility for the product's success. The team started deploying features using A/B tests; a feature was not considered complete until there was accurate data showing the impact of that specific feature on key business metrics. This led everyone to a deeper understanding of how each feature affected overall business performance and dramatically improved the ability of both the product team and the founder to move the business forward.

> **Anna:** This Lean Startup stuff seems to be mostly for small companies.
>
> **M&T:** On the contrary, large companies are finding that Lean Startup ideas work well for new products being developed in their companies. Todd Park, whose story we told in Chapter 1, encouraged government teams to use Lean Startup techniques as they made their data available to the public. Intuit, a $4 billion company highlighted in Chapter 5, encourages product teams to come up with new product ideas and use Lean Startup techniques to test those ideas. General Electric has also publicized its use of Lean Startup practices.[14]
>
> Coauthor Mary worked at 3M, where the mantra "Make a Little, Sell a Little" encouraged product teams to produce, brand, package, and sell small quantities of new products in order to learn what

---

13. Ibid., p. 133.
14. See Beth Comstock and Eric Ries, Lean Startup 2012 video, www.youtube.com/watch?v=TW96_fCSFiU&list=UUQnF0c8GaWDm9T4yMDpGcPA&index=25.

customers wanted and how to make the product successful. So the ideas behind Lean Startup can certainly work in large companies.

Otto: What is a minimum viable product and how do you know when it is ready to launch?

M&T: The point when an idea is ready for public exposure is a judgment call, and it will differ from one domain to the next. Some domains require a complete product that takes years to build; in other domains, a few weeks of work are all that is necessary before a trial release.

Perhaps the best way to see this is to look at the development process of Spotify, a Swedish startup company. In the next section you will see how Spotify begins by focusing on a product design that they believe customers will love. Once they are satisfied with the design, a simple version of the product is built and tested internally; this is the minimum viable product. When the MVP is considered good enough to go public, it is made available to a small subset of customers and a series of Build-Measure-Learn cycles are used to test and improve the product. These cycles create an increasingly better product, until finally it is judged ready to release to all customers. After release to all customers, the product continues to be improved using Build-Measure-Learn cycles until it has grown into a robust product.

Build the Right Thing: Spotify

Spotify is a digital music-streaming service launched in Sweden in October 2008. It gives consumers access to millions of songs on multiple devices and pays artists and rights holders whose music is accessed by consumers. It is a rapidly growing company that currently employs several hundred people in its Stockholm offices. Our sincere thanks go to Henrik Kniberg for writing and illustrating this account of how Spotify builds products.

How Spotify Builds Products

Written and illustrated by Henrik Kniberg[15]

Product development isn't easy. In fact, most product development efforts fail, and the most common reason for failure is building the wrong product.

Spotify is a Swedish lean startup with an awesome track record of product delivery. Their products are loved by users and artists and spread virally—they have over 20 million active users, 5 million paying subscribers, and are growing fast. For example, it took roughly a year to go from zero to 1 million paying subscribers in the United States, a foreign market with plenty of established players.

The products are designed to be easy, personal, and fun. Here's the paradox, though: Successful companies like Spotify only want to deliver products that people love. But they don't know if people love a product until they've delivered it.

So how do they do it? This section will provide a high-level summary of Spotify's approach to product development.

Summary

Our core philosophy is:

- We create innovative products while managing risk by prototyping early and cheaply.
- We don't launch on date; we launch on quality.
- We ensure that our products go from being great at launch to becoming amazing by relentlessly tweaking after launch.

All major product initiatives go through four stages: "Think It," "Build It," "Ship It," and "Tweak It." Figure 4-3 illustrates the flow from idea to product and what comes out of each stage along the way.

---

15. Disclaimer: Like all models, this is a simplification of reality. We don't always follow this process to the letter, and there is a lot of local variation. But this article should give you the general idea.

The material in this article is based on discussions with Gustav Söderström, Oskar Stål, Olof Carlson, and their internal documents and frameworks such as the "Think It, Build It, Ship It, Tweak It" framework. I also learned a lot by talking to designers, developers, and agile coaches. Thanks, everyone!

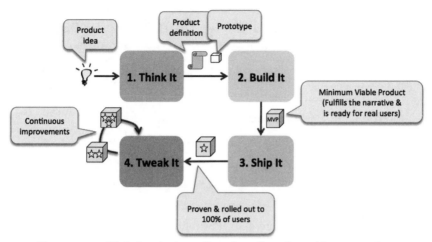

Figure 4-3 High-level view of product flow from idea to product

- **Think It** = figure out what type of product we are building and why.
- **Build It** = create a minimum viable product that is ready for real users.
- **Ship It** = gradually roll out to 100% of all users while measuring and improving.
- **Tweak It** = continuously improve the product. This is really an end state; the product stays in Tweak It until it is shut down or reimagined (= back to Think It).

Spotify has over 30 squads[16] and a number of different products, so to keep track of what's going on and visualize it to the rest of the company, we use a product status board that shows which products are in which stage. Figure 4-4 shows roughly how the board looks.

We are also experimenting with forecasting mechanisms, with squads providing a regularly updated date range (date X–date Y) for when they think their product will reach the next stage.

Why Four Stages?

The biggest risk is building the wrong product—a product that doesn't delight our users or doesn't improve success metrics such as user acquisition, user retention, and so on. We call this "product risk."

---

16. A squad is a small, cross-functional, self-organizing development team. For more information, see "Scaling Agile @ Spotify with Tribes, Squads, Chapters, and Guilds," posted at http://blog.crisp.se/2012/11/14/henrikkniberg/scaling-agile-at-spotify.

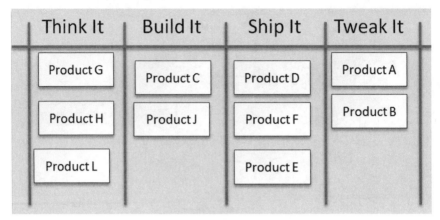

Figure 4-4   Portfolio board

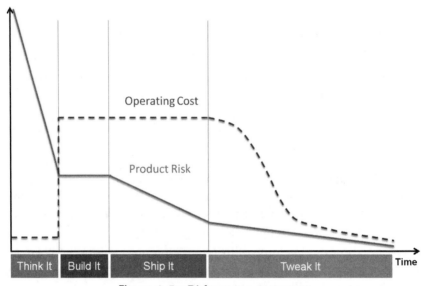

Figure 4-5   Risk-versus-cost curve
for four-stage model of product development

The four-stage model helps us effectively drive down risk and get products out the door quickly. Figure 4-5 shows how product risk (solid line) is reduced at each stage and how cost-intensive each stage is (dashed line).

As you can see, the Think It stage drives down risk at a low cost. You can also see why we want to shorten the Build It stage as much as possible (high operating cost and little risk reduction). The gradually reduced

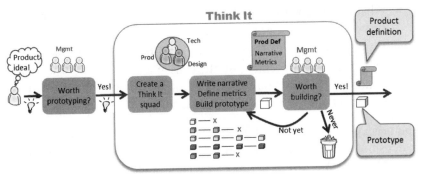

Figure 4-6   The Think It stage

operating cost in Tweak It reflects that, over time, the product doesn't need to be updated as much and squads can start moving on to other things.

The duration of each stage varies a lot; the ratios above are just an example. The total time varies too; some products get to production within a few months, but others take a half year or more. Within each stage, though, releases (even if only internal) are done on a fairly continuous basis.

So, let's take a closer look at each stage.

Think It

Product ideas are born all the time and can come from anyone in the company. Most ideas are improvements to existing products ("tweaks"), and the squads will simply implement and release these on their own.

The Think It stage (Figure 4-6) is for when someone comes up with a whole new product idea or wants to reimagine an existing product.

If management agrees that the idea is worth exploring, a small, cross-functional Think It squad is formed. This typically consists of a developer, a designer, and a product leader. Their job is to write a product definition and build a compelling prototype.

The product definition is a short document that answers questions such as these:

- Why should we build this? Who will benefit from this and how?
- What are the key metrics that we expect this product to improve? This could be measured in terms of how much music is streamed, how many downloads, how many logins, and so forth.

- What are the hypotheses? How will we know if this product is successful?

- Is this a "step change" (that is, a product that we expect will give at least a 2x improvement on the chosen metric)? If we expect only minor improvement on the metrics, there had better be some other strong reason for building it—for example, a strategic reason.

The product definition is not a requirements document or a project plan. It does not contain lists of features, budgets, resource plans, and such. It is more like a data-driven purpose statement. The most important part of the product definition is the narrative. What story are we going to tell the world? What will the press release look like?

For example, here's an excerpt from a short video presenting a narrative for Spotify's "Discover" tab:

> **Introducing a better way to discover music.**
>
> Look! Your favorite artist just shared a song with you. We're bringing artists and fans closer than ever before. Like an artist? Just follow them, and share your discoveries with friends.

The key thing here is that the narrative is written before the product is built! That way we make sure that the product is compelling before we even build it.

In addition, the Think It squad builds lots of different prototypes to experiment with the look and feel of this product—both "lo-fi" paper prototypes and "hi-fi" runnable prototypes (but with fake data sources and such). Internal focus groups are used to help figure out which prototypes best convey the narrative until we've narrowed them down to just a few winning candidates.

This is an iterative process with no deadline. The product is simply not worth building until we can show a compelling narrative and a runnable prototype that fulfills it, and we can't decide up front how long that will take.

As illustrated in the risk-versus-cost curve, the Think It stage lets us drive down product risk in a very cost-effective way—we are just prototyping and experimenting. This gives us a cheap and safe way to fail, so we can keep trying until we find out what the right product is to build.

Definition of Done: The Think It stage ends when management and the squad jointly believe that the product is worth building (or that the product will never be worth building and should be discarded).

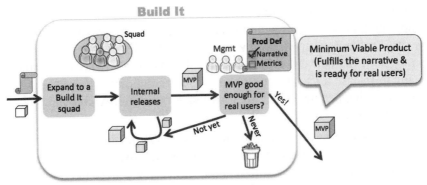

Figure 4-7   The Build It stage

| Unusable product (embarrassing) | Minimum Viable Product (lovable but limited) | Complete product (expensive) |

Figure 4-8   Minimum viable product

This is a subjective decision, with no hard data to support it. The hard data comes in the Ship It stage, so we want to get there as quickly as possible.

Build It

The Think It squad is now expanded to form a more permanent squad (sometimes multiple squads), with all the skills needed to build, test, and ship the real product. This squad will own the product over the long term, not just during Build It.

The goal of the Build It stage (Figure 4-7) is to build an MVP that is good enough to be released to external users and good enough to prove something about the product. The MVP is built iteratively using agile software development methods such as Scrum, Kanban, and Extreme Programming.

There is a balance to be found here, illustrated on the useless-to-perfect scale in Figure 4-8.

On the one hand, we don't want to build a complete product before shipping it, because that would delay our learning. We can't be sure that we are on the right track until we've delivered real software to real users, so we want to get there as quickly as possible. On the other hand, we don't want to release a useless or embarrassing product. Even if we say it is a beta or alpha, people expect great software from Spotify and judge us by what we release.

So the squad needs to figure out the smallest possible thing they can build to fulfill the basic narrative and delight the users. We need it to be narrative complete, not feature complete. Perhaps a better term is *minimum lovable product*. A bicycle is a lovable and useful product for somebody with no better means of transport, but it is still very far from the motorcycle that it will evolve into. We do need to fulfill the basic narrative, though, or our measurements will be misleading: "Hey, we released a wheel, and nobody used it, so the product is a failure and we shouldn't build the rest of the bike!"

The key difference between Think It and Build It is that in Think It, we take all the shortcuts we can and don't worry about technical quality. In Build It, we strive to write production-level code and build quality in.

Definition of Done: The Build It stage ends when management and the squad jointly believe that the product fulfills the basic narrative and is good enough to start releasing to real users.

We are ready for the Moment of Truth!

Ship It

The purpose of the Ship It stage (Figure 4-9) is to gradually roll out the product to 100% of the users while measuring and ensuring that the product fulfills its promise out in the wild.

The squad starts by releasing to a small percentage of all users (typically 1% to 5%) in order to collect data. How do those users act compared to the other 95% to 99%?

Remember, in the Think It stage we defined a few hypotheses for the product. Now we can finally test whether those hypotheses hold true and iteratively improve the product as necessary. We'll rarely get it right on the first try, and part of the strength in this model is that we don't have to.

When management and the squad agree that the product is having the intended impact on the small user group, we gradually roll it out to more users while still measuring and improving. This gives us time to deal with operational aspects such as hardware capacity, monitoring, deployment scripts, scalability, and other factors.

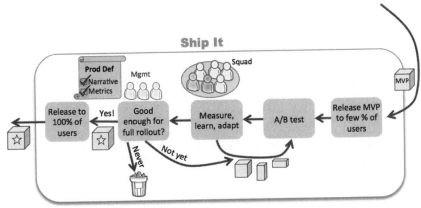

Figure 4-9 The Ship It stage

Definition of Done: The Ship It stage ends when the product is available to all users.

Note that the product is still not "feature complete"; finishing Ship It just means that the product (MVP + necessary improvements) has been 100% rolled out. There is no such thing as "feature complete," since the product continuously evolves even after Ship It.

Tweak It

The Tweak It stage (Figure 4-10) is the most important stage, since this is where all products end up (unless they get trashed along the way), and the place where products spend most of their time.

The product is now in production and available to all users. Although it has proven itself to a certain extent in the Ship It stage, there is always plenty of room for improvement. The squad continues to experiment and A/B test and improve the product while following up on the metrics. This can include significant new features as well as minor tweaks.

Sometime in the future, however, the squad may reach a point of diminishing returns for the product. The product is great, the most important improvements have been made, and the cost/benefit ratio of new feature development is less attractive. Looking at the metrics, new features and improvements don't seem to be moving the needle a lot. This means the product is approaching a "local maximum" (see Figure 4-11).

At this point the squad and management will discuss: *Are we happy being at the top of this hill, or is there a higher peak to be found?* In the former case, the squad may gradually move on to other products. In the latter case, the squad may go back to Think It to reimagine this product

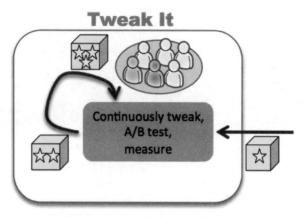

Figure 4-10 The Tweak It stage

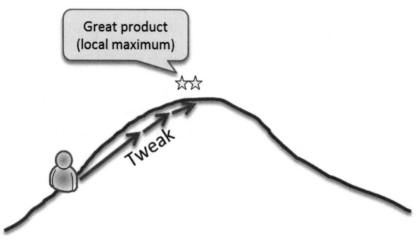

Figure 4-11 Local maximum

and make a leap for the global maximum (or at least a higher peak . . .). (See Figure 4-12.)

One example of this is the spotify.com Web site. The Web site was tweaked for four years before we decided to rethink it in the summer of 2012. The Web site now conveys the Spotify vision in a completely different and dramatically more effective way.

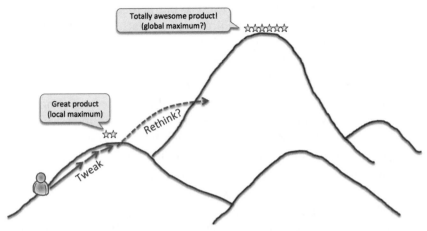

Figure 4-12   Reimagining a product

Final Words

Final Words

If some parts of this model made you think, "Duh, I already knew that, we've been doing that for decades," you're probably right. This model isn't about New and Amazing, it is just about Stuff That Works—new or old doesn't really matter. I find this combination of practices to be very inspiring and powerful, and I hope you find something that could be useful in your context.

Questions to Ponder

1. How does your organization decide what features a product team should work on next? How do you know that those decisions actually make sense?

2. Can you—and do you—create a hypothesis about the value of proposed features? Do you validate that features are delivering that value once deployed?

3. How long does it take from the time you decide to make a normal priority change until the change gets through your scheduling system, your queues, your work system, your validation and deployment system, and to your customers?

4. How far apart are your releases? What percent of a release cycle is spent "hardening" the product—validating that it works as expected and fixing any problems that are found? What are you doing to drive that below 10%?

5. Are your estimates single numbers, or are they ranges? Why?

6. You can either manage to deadline and let scope vary (Ericsson Case 1), or you can manage to scope and let deadline vary (Ericsson Case 2). But not both. Which makes more sense for your environment? Which do you actually do?

7. Consider two teams: Team 1 delivers five features that are exactly what your customers want. Team 2 takes 50% longer and delivers ten features, five of which are the same ones Team 1 delivered, plus five more features that may be useful to customers in the future. Which team is more efficient? Which product is more efficient? Why?

8. Do you organize around projects or products? Does this organization affect your batch sizes? The length of your release cycles? The number of things a person is expected to work on at the same time? The amount of work-in-progress?

9. What methods or organizational structure do you use to ensure the long-term integrity of your product architecture? What methods or organizational structure do you use to ensure rapid delivery of competitive product features? How are these two goals balanced in your organization?

10. Does everyone on a product team feel responsible for the product's business success? Do product teams do A/B testing? Limited releases? Canary rollouts?

5

Breakthrough Innovation

Seeing the Future

After 50 years of steady growth, the revenues of American newspapers suddenly fell off a cliff, as Figure 5-1 shows. Newspapers around the world suffered a similar fate. The reason is clear: Advertising fled from

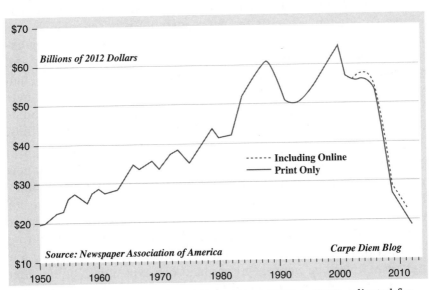

Figure 5-1 Newspaper advertising revenue 1950 to 2012, adjusted for inflation.[1]

1. From "Carpe Diem," Professor Mark J. Perry's Blog for Economics and Finance, October 5, 2012, http://mjperry.blogspot.com/2012/09/freefall-adjusted-for-inflation-print.html. Used with permission.

print media and moved online. Newspaper classified sections, once a highly profitable revenue generator, have largely disappeared. These days, people prefer to search the Internet rather than scan pages and pages of tiny print ads when they are looking for jobs or cars or used merchandise. You can argue that newspapers should have seen the threat coming and done something about it, but the fact is that very few newspapers were alert enough to see the threat to their lucrative classified advertising business in time to defend it. However, there is at least one very notable exception: Schibsted Media Group.

Case: FINN.no

In 1996 a group of five local newspapers in Norway formed an alliance (now called Schibsted Media Group) to meet the Internet challenge. Think back to 1996: The World Wide Web was barely three years old and was accessed by a dial-up modem. Yahoo! and eBay were small California startups. Not too many newspapers saw the Internet as a threat, but this collection of Norwegian newspapers took it seriously.

The Oslo newspaper *Aftenposten* initiated a project aimed at defending the print revenue of the affiliated newspapers. The project produced a Web site, Aftenposten Visavisen, which was bundled into the existing newspaper business rather than assigned dedicated staffing. The experiment was a failure, and Schibsted learned what experts in disruptive technologies had just begun preaching: Disruptive new businesses have a better chance at success if they are formed as separate business units rather than embedded in existing product lines.

So when Schibsted tried to establish an online presence again in 2000, it formed a separate entity with a dedicated organization, new people, and a new culture. The new business unit had a new brand—FINN.no—and was chartered to attack a key source of revenue for the group's newspapers: classified ads. Nevertheless, the newspapers supported the new subsidiary, advertising its presence and touting its superiority in their classified pages. "Our investors, especially our American investors, were skeptical about our exposure in online after the dotcom bubble burst and advised us to stick with the traditional media," said FINN.no CEO Christian Printzell Halvorsen, "but luckily we ignored their advice."

In 2001, 2% of Schibsted's revenue and virtually no profits came from online activity; by 2012, 40% of revenue and 65% of profits came from its online business. Unlike almost every other newspaper group in the world, Schibsted is doing very well financially. A quick look at some numbers gives an idea of just how well.

FINN.no is Norway's second- or third-largest Web site. Its brand is recognized by 96% of the Norwegian population. In Norway, FINN.no holds the number-one position in online job postings, real estate, cars, general merchandise, and display advertising and holds the number-two position in travel and services. It has at least 2.5 million unique visitors a week. In 2012 there were 550,524,830 visits to FINN.no, or 110 visits per Norwegian, and over the year an average Norwegian spent 21 hours on the site. There were 3.8 million ads worth a total of 562 billion NOKs posted in 2012; this is equal to a whopping 20+% of Norway's GDP!

You have to wonder why more newspapers around the world didn't see the Internet threat coming and do something about it early, before online competitors took over their classified markets. Halvorsen says: "It's easier to act before the market changes than to play catch-up after. A willingness to cannibalize our own revenues has made Schibsted a global leader in transforming from traditional media to online."

So the trick is to detect early signals of a disruption and act quickly, even if that means attacking some of the most important revenue streams of the company. No wonder this is difficult! But as the Schibsted Media Group discovered, it's better to disrupt yourself than to be disrupted by competitors. Halvorsen notes, "Disruptive innovation is not only a way to transformation, but to entirely new revenue streams." Today FINN.no has seven growing vertical markets, a couple of which are completely new, giving the company revenue streams that would never have been available to the print media.

Disruptive Innovation

The concept of disruptive technologies was introduced in a 1995 *Harvard Business Review* article, "Disruptive Technologies: Catching the Wave" by Joseph Bower and Clayton Christensen.[2] The authors showed how the success of established companies and their most popular products attracts competitors. These competitors often develop products that are less expensive, or smaller, or require less power, or are easier

---

2. This was followed by the classic work on disruptive technologies, *The Innovator's Dilemma* by Clayton Christensen, which was originally published in 1997 by Harvard Business School Press.

to use than the established products. At first the new products don't meet the needs of existing customers, so the incumbent companies are not concerned.

Once disruptive technologies gain a customer base—usually outside the existing customer base—they grow stronger and more competent while maintaining the cost or size or power or ease-of-use advantage that got them into the market in the first place. Often it's just a matter of time before these disruptive products take over the market from the established leaders. The remarkable thing is that while the upstarts are growing strong, incumbents usually ignore them. It's as if the established companies have blinders on and simply cannot see what is happening.

Wikipedia did not invent the idea of an encyclopedia; it just stumbled on a faster, cheaper way of compiling one. It took a long time for people used to reading articles written by experts to begin to trust a crowd-sourced compilation of knowledge, so existing encyclopedia publishers didn't take Wikipedia seriously at first. But today those encyclopedias are no longer published.

Amazon.com did not invent the need for companies to have fast, easy, scalable access to servers on demand; it developed the capability to serve its own needs, then found a way to provide its internal services to others at a very attractive price point. It took a long time for companies to begin to consider moving storage systems to the cloud, but new companies that were just getting started and didn't have any corporate servers yet found that Amazon Web Services provided just what they were looking for.

Some new technologies don't fit the classic definition of a disruptive technology because there are no incumbents to disrupt. Instead, an entrepreneur has a frustrating experience and imagines how a new technology might get the job done better, faster, or cheaper than the current annoying way of doing things. She exploits the technology, solves the problem, and sets out to sell the new approach to all those people who are trying to do the same job using the old, frustrating methods.

Who knew that we wanted to upload videos to the Web so we could connect with family, friends, and colleagues? But as camera phones became increasingly capable of taking videos, a pent-up demand developed for a way to share the videos—and YouTube was born to solve that problem. Who would have guessed that so many people would be willing to write reviews of books and hotels and photography gear, and that individual purchasing decisions would evolve to depend far more on consumer ratings than on marketing efforts?

Another form of disruptive technology is big-bang disruption,[3] which occurs when a new technology is adopted so quickly that it kills a whole category of products in a matter of months or even weeks. For example, when free navigation apps appeared on smartphones, makers of specialized navigation devices such as TomTom, Garmin, and Magellan saw a huge percentage of their customer base disappear almost immediately—at the high end as well as the low end of their product lines. Not only were navigation apps free, they were updated frequently and integrated into other smartphone apps, so they not only cost less, but they outperformed existing navigation devices from the beginning. These kinds of game-changing technologies are not really aimed at displacing market incumbents; often they emerge from completely unrelated areas. Nevertheless, big-bang disruption can trigger instant defections and leave no time for incumbents to react.

The list of disrupted market segments is long and growing fast—film, pay phones, movie rental stores, long-distance phone calls, phone books, travel guidebooks, maps, dictionaries, cameras, and on and on. Very few businesses are immune from the threat. And yet, when a market segment is disrupted, it is rare that the disrupter is an incumbent. It's almost as if successful companies don't spend the time to ask themselves if there might be a better way to solve their customers' problems.

 Otto: I've seen a lot of companies disrupted out of business, but it always happens to someone else. I'd like to think that my company is doing the best job it possibly can at serving our customers.

M&T: The theory is that you want to disrupt yourself before someone disrupts you. In practice, this is not easy because you are focusing so intensely on making your business successful that you don't see the weak signal buried in the noise of keeping today's business running.

Focus

 Focus. It's a lesson we learn as youngsters. Focus to get good grades. Focus to make good decisions. When we want to do something well, we learn that if we practice hard and focus on the details, we will get better.

---

3. See Larry Downes and Paul Nunes, "Big-Bang Disruption," *Harvard Business Review*, March 2013.

Companies that are large and successful have learned how to focus on execution. The organizational structure, the metrics, and the culture have evolved together and reinforce each other in a way that leads to excellent operations. Continuing to improve requires a laser focus on optimizing key operational metrics such as productivity, quality, and customer satisfaction. Improvement involves understanding problems and capturing their essence, zooming in on the details, weighing the alternatives, and finding the right solution. In fact, this approach works very well—at least for well-defined problems.

A laser focus on execution gives you the best possible solutions for the problems you are trying to solve, but it will not tell you if they are the right problems. You will get the right answers to the questions you ask, but you will not know if you are asking the right questions. In fact, an intense focus on operations distracts you from realizing that there are other areas of risk, other opportunities that you are not seeing. For business-as-usual situations, operational excellence is critical, and good companies have mastered it. But when there is a discontinuity in the business environment—an order-of-magnitude change in one of the factors in the marketplace—focusing on immediate problems blinds you to the fact that things have changed, that business is no longer "as usual."

 Anna: Our business operates in a well-defined market with well-defined problems, and focus is one thing we're good at. **M&T:** Being very good at what you do makes it difficult to see changes in your market. The more focused you are, the stronger your confirmation bias is likely to be. You will see what you are looking for and miss what doesn't fit your mental model. If this can happen at Intel, it can happen to you.

Case: Intel's Near-Death Experience

Andy Grove of Intel is one of the few CEOs who led his company successfully through the crisis of a disruptive technology and survived to write a book about it.[4] The story begins in 1984, when Intel's memory business started to slow down. Japanese manufacturers were selling memory chips of equivalent quality at lower prices than Intel. At that time, the people at Intel felt that their company *was* memory; it got its

---

4. Andrew S. Grove, *Only the Paranoid Survive: How to Exploit the Crisis Points That Challenge Every Company* (Doubleday Business, 1996).

start as a memory company in 1968 and had competed fiercely in the market ever since. Everything else the company made was peripheral; memory got the greatest share of the R&D budget because everyone "knew" that memory was the company's technology driver. The reason Intel made other products—microprocessors, for instance—was because everyone "knew" that customers would want to buy a complete product line from one supplier.

After fighting a frustrating and losing battle against low-cost memory from Japan for over a year, Grove, then COO, asked CEO Gordon Moore:

> "If we got kicked out and the board brought in a new CEO, what do you think he would do?" Gordon answered without hesitation, "He would get us out of memories." I stared at him, numb, then said, "Why shouldn't you and I walk out the door, come back and do it ourselves?"[5]

At that point Grove knew intellectually what had to be done, but he found it almost impossible to make it happen. Leaders debated endlessly, steps in the right direction were timid, and halfway measures were making things worse. It took a full year after his memorable discussion with Moore for Grove to finally build up the courage to announce to the world that Intel was exiting the memory business. By that time the reaction from customers was "It sure took you a long time."

It took another year before Intel turned the corner and became profitable again. Three years is a long time to make a change in a fast-moving industry, and Intel was almost too late. But it was able to leave its past behind and become an even stronger microprocessor company, while few of its former competitors survived.

Intel was fortunate; when memory failed to sustain the company, it could fall back on microprocessors. The story of how microprocessors just "happened" to be available as a fallback position gives some hints for how to survive in a world of disruptive technologies.

Early in Intel's history, a young sales engineer named Ted Hoff was helping a Japanese customer named BUSICOM design a chip for a calculator. Hoff thought he could design something that would go beyond BUSICOM's specifications and solve their whole problem. Encouraged by then-CEO Robert Noyce and aided by Stanley Mazor, Hoff

---

5. Ibid., p. 89.

completed the design of the 4004 microprocessor and sold the idea to BUSICOM executives. (They needed convincing.) Federico Faggin was hired to engineer the new chip, and he prepared it for manufacturing in record time. Intel introduced the 4004—the world's first single-chip microprocessor—in 1971.

The microprocessor business grew gradually over the next 15 years. When the memory crisis hit Intel in 1984, microprocessors were clearly the higher-margin product. It was the policy of the production and financial planners at the time to allocate Intel's limited production capacity to the most profitable products. So while the executives were dithering, middle managers "adjusted Intel's strategic posture" by making more and more microprocessors and fewer memory chips. When Grove finally quit focusing on memory and looked around to figure out what to do next, he discovered that Intel had already become a microprocessor company.

 Otto: So the lesson is to do a lot of things at once, not just one?

M&T: There are several lessons here: Encourage eager engineers to follow their passion. Expect front-line people to understand and solve a customer's whole problem. Invest in new ideas that may take over a decade to bear fruit. And set up a system that expects local managers to have the wisdom and gives them the freedom to do the right thing.

 Anna: I would think that the Intel executives should have seen the value of microprocessors. Wasn't that their job?

M&T: Andy Grove wrote that when there is a 10× change in some factor in the marketplace—he calls this a "strategic inflection point"—the company's executives will always be the last to know.[6] They are too busy losing sleep over saving the business they have struggled to make successful.

Case: A Creative Culture at Pixar

There are a few industries in which senior management is much more likely to lose sleep worrying about creativity than worrying about predictability and efficiency. One of these industries is the film industry. Either a movie is exciting to watch and draws large audiences—or not.

---

6. Grove, *Only the Paranoid Survive.*

Of course it's important for the movie to be high quality and meet production goals. But creativity comes first.

Arguably one of the most creative film studios in the United States is Pixar Animation Studios, creator of *Toy Story*; *A Bug's Life*; *Monsters, Inc.*; *The Incredibles*; *Up*; *Finding Nemo*; *Cars*; *Ratatouille*; *WALL·E*; *Brave*; and other films. Every year, it seems, an engaging new movie emerges from Pixar to delight audiences. How is it that the studio has been able to generate blockbuster after blockbuster, year after year?

President Ed Catmull set out to answer that question in the article "How Pixar Fosters Collective Creativity." He wrote that well before his company was successful, he had developed a healthy fear of success turning into failure:

> Observing the rise and fall of computer companies during my career has affected me deeply. Many companies put together a phenomenal group of people who produced great products. They had the best engineers, exposure to the needs of customers, access to changing technology, and experienced management. Yet many made decisions at the height of their powers that were stunningly wrongheaded, and they faded into irrelevance. How could really smart people completely miss something so crucial to their survival? I remember asking myself more than once: "If we are ever successful, will we be equally blind?"[7]

Catmull is a computer graphics expert whose lifelong dream was to create the first computer-animated film. With *Toy Story*, he realized that dream, so he began to search for a new challenge. He decided his next goal would be to build a studio that had the depth, robustness, and perseverance to enable it to produce spectacular movies long after he and the other founders retired. From observing the failures of his colleagues in the computer industry, he concluded that he should focus on creating a great culture in which creativity would flourish.

At Pixar, the culture starts with the insight that creativity is not a solo act; it involves a large number of people from different disciplines working effectively together, constantly solving problems. And that's not easy. "Getting people in different disciplines to treat one another as peers is just as important as getting people within disciplines to do so. But it's much harder," Catmull writes.[8] Different disciplines have

---

7. "How Pixar Fosters Collective Creativity," *Harvard Business Review* 86, no. 9 (September 2008).
8. Ibid.

different languages and customs, and within any organization there always seems to be one function that considers itself to be more favored than the others. Catmull was determined that this would not happen at Pixar. He took the unprecedented step of making sure that software experts and creative leads had equal pay and equal status.

But that was only the beginning. In most studios, there is a development department chartered to come up with movie concepts. At Pixar, the main job of the development department is, instead, to assemble teams of people who work well together, who address problems effectively and make steady progress, and who bring out the best in each other. The job of executives is to create a climate that fosters respect and trust and unleashes creative energy, because, Catmull believes, this is the kind of atmosphere where passion and dedication flourish, and people are eager to go to work every day because they know they are a part of something amazing.

Pixar University is a key element of developing mutual respect. Here everyone is encouraged to develop skills in other disciplines. In any given class there will be experts honing their skills alongside novices from other areas of the company. In this way people work together in friendly environments, learn to appreciate the work of their colleagues from other disciplines, and bring a broader set of alternatives to bear on mutual problems.

The Pixar Organization

Catmull believes that the creative vision behind a great movie comes from one or two people, not from executives and certainly not from a development department. So each movie has a director who has complete creative authority, with the understanding that a director's job is to guide and inspire a team of 200 to 250 people with a unifying vision. Working closely with the director is a producer who is responsible for things such as budget and schedule and who is expected to understand how to leverage such constraints to enhance creativity.

Teams have daily meetings in which members show their work in its unfinished state and receive feedback from the director and other team members. This has the same effect as continuous integration in software development—it keeps people from heading down the wrong path and eliminates integration surprises. There is a "brain trust" of directors with a proven track record of great films who regularly review the state of each film, making suggestions for improvement, but never interfering with the autonomy of the director, who is free to adopt or ignore the advice.

To keep the company on track over time, there is a postmortem process in which the successful and not so successful practices of a film are discussed in order to keep the studio on a path of improvement. Executives encourage new people to challenge ingrained practices and come up with new ideas. In the end, Catmull believes Pixar's organizational structures and practices should be designed and continually redesigned to support its culture—a culture that creates deep respect and trust between people.

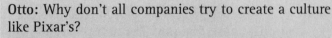

Otto: Why don't all companies try to create a culture like Pixar's?

M&T: Once companies reach a certain size, they tend to shift their focus from developing new, creative products to making and delivering the products they already have as efficiently as possible. Think of the difference between a chef and a cook: A chef is expected to try lots of things and come up with creative new dishes; cooks are then expected to make that dish efficiently and with little variation. When companies focus on the cooking part of the business—operations—they tend to lose sight of the fact that they need to constantly come up with new recipes and neglect to maintain the culture necessary for creativity to flourish. But as we move into an era when consumer experience is a critically important selling factor for many products, a creative culture will become increasingly important.

Change the Focus

Sometime in the next decade or two, a disruptive technology is likely to threaten your industry. When you think about it, this is probably your biggest risk in the long run. So what can you do to be prepared?

Your safest bet is to spend some time looking outward instead of inward. Instead of looking for solutions to problems, step back and ask yourself whether you are working on the right problems, the important problems. Are you worried about how to be more efficient? More predictable? More productive? Has it occurred to you that these may be the wrong questions if a disruptive technology is headed your way?

. . . From Productivity to Impact

How can my organization be more productive? We hear this question all the time, and it's a frustrating question, because productivity isn't the right thing to worry about—at least in product development. Asking software developers to write more code is like asking authors to put more words in their books or teachers to put more children in their classrooms. When creativity and learning are important, focusing on quantity makes no sense. And yet in one of the most creative, learning-focused professions we know of—software development—the question we get most often is *How will lean or agile methods increase productivity?* Quite frankly, that is the wrong question.

The path to effective software development is not increasing productivity; it is developing the essential features that customers will love—and only those features. The more features you add to a code base, the more complexity you add with it. The more complexity you add, the more difficult and expensive the code base is to change. In more cases than you can imagine, the features and the complexity are not really necessary. So the best attitude to adopt is that lines of code are bad. Function points are bad. Even stories and features are bad. Instead of worrying about how to develop stuff faster, it is far better to learn how to stop developing the things that are not important and focus on the things that will have real impact.

Let us give you some examples. We used to work with companies in Scandinavia that were developing user interfaces for cell phones using a two-year-long waterfall process. We urged them to switch to a more rapid process, and they probably did. But that didn't change the fact that everything they were working on became obsolete the day the iPhone was introduced. We ran into a bank that was proud it took only a year to develop a mobile app that could display account balances. But that didn't change the fact that a competing bank provided full banking services on mobile phones before the first bank even started its development effort.

We worked with a CIO at a financial services company who was trying to figure out how to do everything in his annual budget plan plus satisfy all of the new requests that came in during the year. He was unwilling to deal with the fact that a large amount of the stuff in his budget was no longer needed. If he had promised to deliver something during annual budgeting, it had to be delivered, needed or not. With that kind of logic, we weren't surprised when his company suffered huge losses in the banking crash of 2008. We noticed that Handelsbanken in Sweden fared much better in the downturn and were reminded of the IT people in one of our classes who came from a Handelsbanken branch. The bank expects branches to be responsible for their own information systems, and we assure you the people in our class would not have been expected to waste their time on development that was unlikely to contribute to their branch's success.

Consider General Motors (GM). After years of outsourcing IT to lower costs, it initiated a dramatic shift to insourced IT in 2012.[9] Why? Executives wanted IT to be more responsive, more creative, to bring more value to the business units. This is not to say that IT will have a larger budget; it will have a budget commensurate with the value it delivers. The thing that GM recognized is that the best way to cut the IT budget is not to do more with less, but to do less of the stuff that does not need to be done and focus on the stuff that has real impact.

If you don't have enough time to do everything in your pipeline, you should suspect that this is probably not a productivity problem; it is almost certainly a pipeline problem. Let us be clear: We believe that business objectives should be met within whatever time and budget constraints the objectives are worth. But the thing is, the way to achieve a software objective within a time and budget constraint is almost always going to be to write less code. The way to get a product developed on time and on budget is to develop fewer features—just make sure that they are the right features. Pixar has a wise saying: *A movie is never finished, it's released.* Similarly, software is never finished, it's released.

When people are overworked in a development organization, it's safe to assume that their managers are not doing a good job of deciding what's really important. Once, for example, we worked with an insurance company that was developing software to support a new call center. Things were behind schedule, and we strongly recommended that they remove features. An effort was made to do so, but it was politically difficult, so not much was removed. Instead, the senior developers were offered a huge incentive to get an impossibly long list of features done in time for a politically important release date. The developers coded furiously, ignoring testing, and the features were delivered, full of bugs, in time to meet the release date. Bonuses were paid. And the development team spent the next year cleaning up the mess, while the call center limped along with an unreliable system. The developers were not proud of their work. "Couldn't some features have been removed so you could have delivered high-quality software?" we asked the lead developers. "Certainly! Half the features we delivered aren't being used and never will be," we were told. But promises had

---

9. Rob Preston, "General Motors Will Slash Outsourcing in IT Overhaul," *InformationWeek,* July 9, 2012.

been made, and the overwhelming need to keep those promises prevented the sensible approach of limiting features and delivering high-quality software on time.

Disruptive competitors have less time, less money, and fewer experts than you have. You can be sure that they are not going to waste their valuable time and money worrying about productivity. They are going to figure out a way to get the job done by doing less stuff and delivering more of what customers really want. When this happens, you will have very little to show for all of your work.

Anna: It sounds like you don't believe in productivity.
M&T: Peter Drucker once said, "There is nothing quite so useless as doing with great efficiency something that should not be done at all." The best way to be productive is to be sure first of all that you are doing the right thing. Every bit of time spent "productively" doing the wrong thing is wasted time. Service organizations, for example, often measure productivity by measuring the time it takes to respond to complaints. They could be far more productive in the long run if they spent time trying to find and eliminate the root cause of each complaint—even though that would take more time per complaint.

. . . From Predictability to Experimentation

In his book *Adapt*,[10] Tim Harford notes that the path to long-term survival in a complex system is simple, well known, and proven: (1) Create variation, (2) select what succeeds, and (3) repeat. Harford points out that the first step—variation—will necessarily produce failures as well as successes. If there are no failures, there is no effective variation, so it is necessary to accept the fact that failure will happen and therefore to make failure acceptable. It is also necessary to be sure that no failure will be catastrophic, so a series of small experiments is often preferable to a single large change. "When an evolutionary process is let loose upon a problem, it will often find solutions that no human designer would have dreamed of," Harford says.

One way to ensure that your company is positioned to survive over the long term is to become comfortable using evolutionary processes to constantly adapt. Learn how to experiment by placing small bets and pursuing the ones that work. Tolerate failure but make sure it's

---

10. Tim Harford, *Adapt: Why Success Always Starts with Failure* (Picador, 2012).

survivable, make sure it's recognizable, and kill it quickly. And be prepared to scale quickly when an experiment proves to be extraordinarily successful.

As an example, Google is able to leverage its service-based delivery model to make large-scale experimentation the basis of its research.[11] Small research teams have access to the power of many internal services, which simplifies the processes of design, testing, production, and maintenance. Therefore, relatively small teams can quickly create experimental systems to explore new ideas and gain access to a large consumer base to facilitate empirical research. Once new ideas are proven, Google can use the same services to quickly create powerful new products and services.

Welcome Surprises

 "If you never fail, you are not trying hard enough," coauthor Mary was often told when she worked at 3M. The story of almost every blockbuster 3M product started with a surprise result from some sort of experiment—a market trial with strange results, a chemistry formula that didn't do what it was supposed to do, a frustrated customer. Surprises were not considered failures, but a message that by digging deeper there might be a gem to be found. Surprises were the beginning of quite a few major lines of business.

People at innovative companies know that the best way to understand a complex system is to stimulate it in a way that they expect will move it in a particular direction and then observe whether or not they were right. They know that the more small experiments they do, the more they learn. They understand that if their experiments never fail, they aren't learning anything new. They realize that the biggest advances in knowledge start out as surprises.

And yet, most companies are not structured to accept surprises; they tend to focus on predictability, not on surprises. Their systems and metrics are aimed at flawless execution, not on running experiments that might fail. In companies where every investment is measured against a hurdle and everyone's career depends on never being associated with failure, no one is going to take any risks.

---

11. Alfred Spector, Peter Norvig, and Slav Petrov, "Google's Hybrid Approach to Research," *Communications of the ACM* 55, no. 7 (July 2012).

Innovative companies, on the other hand, have a portfolio of risky ideas that are in various states of investigation and development. There is no expectation that they will all succeed—and in fact if they do, the company realizes that it is not learning very much. Managers at innovative companies know that opportunity lies in the surprises uncovered when exploring unknown territory. So they put in place a culture that encourages people to try new things and does not penalize failure. They make sure that systems are in place to capitalize on surprises—both good and bad surprises—when they occur. They figure it's better to uncover the weak signals and act on them before nimble competitors close off the opportunity.

Anna: I don't see why we should waste time on experiments that are going to fail. Why can't we figure out in advance what will succeed and what will fail and invest money only in the ideas that will succeed?

M&T: You can do a great job of improving your current products for your current customers with that approach, but it is not going to help you with disruptive innovation. There are a lot of companies that have disappeared or are in trouble because they thought it would be cheaper to predict the future than to invent it.

Experimentation at Intuit

Scott Cook used to work at Procter & Gamble as a brand manager, and years later he joined its board of directors. In the interim, he founded Intuit, a $4 billion company that provides financial software to individuals and small businesses, mostly within the United States. After "retiring" to Intuit's board in 2000, Cook began to look into the unsettling phenomena that so concerned Ed Catmull at Pixar. Why were large, established companies, with all of their brainpower and money, unable to invent successful new disruptive businesses? How did it happen that startups were the ones coming up with all the game-changing innovations? And how could Intuit avoid the fate of the many Silicon Valley success stories that all too quickly disappeared?

Cook set out to examine large companies that had been successful at creating disruptive new businesses in order to look for patterns. He found that there was a common thread running through these companies during their most innovative periods: They had processes in place to encourage small employee teams to conduct frugal experiments.[12]

---

12. *Frugal* means "thrifty" or "economical." See Peter Cohan, "Can Scott Cook Revive Corporate America?" *Forbes,* February 29, 2012, www.forbes.com/sites/petercohan/ 2012/02/29/can-scott-cook-revive-corporate-america/.

In one study, Cook looked at many cases of innovation at Hewlett-Packard and found that in most of these cases, what turned out to be great innovations were initially opposed by CEO David Packard. Nevertheless, they flourished because these three things were true:

- The company "liberated the inventive power of people;"
- It created a "culture of experimentation;" and
- It changed the role of the boss from a decider of whether to pursue or cancel innovation projects to an installer of systems that encourage endless cycles of hypothesis generation, testing with customers, and learning from the gap between quantitative expectations and measured market truth.[13]

Intuit has changed its organizational structure with a bias toward small teams. It has encouraged teams to test out new ideas by quantifying the assumptions that must be true for their idea to become a business success and then quickly running experiments to check out each key assumption. Many innovations have come from this process, ranging from chat areas in tax software, a "Snap Tax" app for cell phones, and a debit card for tax refunds. Perhaps the most interesting one is Fasal, a mobile app that helps farmers in India find better pricing for their produce.

 Case: Fasal Intuit's business has historically been focused on financial systems in the United States, but of course it would like to expand to other countries. In 2008, Bharath Kadaba, a leader of Intuit's development center in India, received a challenge from his boss: *Create new businesses that improve the financial lives of Indians.*[14] Along with the challenge, he received enough funding for about three people—and he wondered how he could meet such a huge challenge with such a small investment. Kadaba recruited a small team led by Deepa Bachu, who had returned home to India after working at Intuit's

---

13. Ibid.
14. From three sources: Talk by Dr. Bharath Kadaba, VP of Engineering and Operations at the Global Business Division of Intuit, at the Lean Startup Conference, San Francisco, December 4, 2012, www.ustream.tv/recorded/27482093/highlight/311462/; "Improving Earning Capacity of Farmers," Case Study by One World Foundation India, http://indiagovernance.gov.in/files/intuit_fasal_edited_intuit_final.pdf; and Austin Carr, "Intuit Taps Text Messages, Economics to Boost Farmer Incomes in India," *Fast Company,* www.fastcoexist.com/1679081/intuit-taps-text-messages-economics-to-boost-farmer-incomes-in-india.

California headquarters for a decade. Bachu was eager to help the neighbors she had grown up with, and her team decided to focus on improving the financial lives of India's 150 million farmers.

In keeping with Intuit's well-known "Follow Me Home" practice, the team spent time visiting farmers and learning about the frustrations they had while running their farming businesses. They found that the biggest frustration was a lack of pricing information for their produce. As vegetables were harvested, farmers did not know which of two or three markets to go to for the best price and had little bargaining power once they arrived with perishable vegetables. The Intuit team believed that the farmers would be helped the most by a system that provided price transparency and helped them decide where to sell their produce. The Intuit team decided that an SMS messaging system would be a good way to accomplish this goal.

At Intuit, when an entrepreneurial team comes up with a novel idea, it is expected to identify the leap-of-faith assumptions behind the idea and test them with quick experiments. The assumptions in this case were that the local buyers would make their prices available and that farmers would be able to use the information. This was not obvious. Why should buyers publicize their prices? And could pricing information really help farmers? Although virtually all farmers had cell phones, they spoke several different languages and many were illiterate.

The experiment to test the critical assumptions was simple and took only days. The engineers chose a single crop in a small area and recruited a dozen or so farmers. They personally contacted the buyers each day for pricing and sent out text messages to the farmers. The results were promising.

Next the team built a minimum viable product—the simplest system that was necessary to get started. It took only 60 days for the engineers to create the first version of a service that was eventually called Fasal. Farmers registered for the service by calling a toll-free number; they were asked about their location, language, and crop details. For the most part, buyers found it valuable to advertise their prices by entering them into the system. In addition, a social network of price collectors was recruited to enter daily prices from the markets. An algorithm determined which prices would be relevant to individual farmers based on the crops they grew. Two or three times a day, the farmers received pricing information and messages from buyers in their own language. Farmers who could not read quickly learned the few words they needed to decipher the messages. Within two weeks, 1,500 farmers were registered on the system, and the team knew it was on the right path. The first experiment was a resounding success, measured not just by the number of farmers but also by the fact that the income of farmers using the system had increased by more than 15%.

The system grew steadily over the next few years, one experiment at a time. By the end of 2012 the team had conducted over 20 major experiments and Fasal had 1.2 million registered farmers, 90% of them active users. It was growing at the rate of 20,000 farmers a week. Why? Farmers found that Fasal increased their income by an average of 20%. "Every farmer, at minimum, is bringing us at least two additional farmers," Bachu says. "So you can start to see the network in place."[15]

The service is free for farmers, and for some time it was funded by Intuit. In fact, there were occasional attempts by senior executives to kill the program, according to Kadaba. "But it was hard to shut them down. Why? Because they were spending so little money."[16] So with minimal funding, the internal startup grew steadily and eventually found a way to make money through advertising in the form of targeted SMS messages.

 Otto: That was a pretty small team—just a few people had to do everything!
M&T: A small team can be a big advantage. When the entire product team is responsible for the product's success, everybody develops a deep understanding of the customers, their lives, their problems, their constraints. The whole team gets involved in each experiment, so people with diverse perspectives imagine, implement, and measure the results of an experiment. Creating small, complete teams inside of the company is a great way to bring a startup mindset to big companies.

. . . *From Efficiency to Decentralization*

Innovative companies are decentralized companies. Generally, decentralization doesn't appear to be the most efficient way to run a company, so companies with serious cost pressures have a tendency to centralize functions and control remote operations more rigorously.

---

15. This quote is from Carr, "Intuit Taps Text Messages."
16. This quote is from Kadaba, Lean Startup Conference.

But the important question to ask is *Where did the cost pressures come from?* Were they always there, or did they arrive unexpectedly? Is it possible that cost pressures are the result of a deeper problem? Might there be an unnoticed change in market dynamics? If this is the case, focusing on efficiency is probably the wrong approach; understanding the essential problem and finding an innovative solution to it will likely yield better results.

When a company comes to believe that innovation is essential to its survival, the time has come to switch its focus from efficiency to decentralization. There are several reasons why decentralization fosters innovation. First of all, it takes a team to field a new product or service, and if a company is structured around independent business teams at multiple locations, innovation has a lot of incubation zones. Second, there is wide agreement that if innovation teams are subject to the same processes and metrics as core business units, they are likely to fail; processes and metrics more suited to a startup business should be used.[17] Third, tightly coupled systems are fragile. A decentralized system is a decoupled system, which can more easily tolerate the failures that go hand in hand with innovation.

Lines of Decentralization

When it comes to promoting innovation in a company, the question is not *Should we decentralize?* The question to ask is *How should we decentralize?* In other words, *Along what lines should decentralization take place?* Decentralization is not a one-size-fits-all affair. Companies need to consider the context of their industry and markets to understand the best approach to decentralization. Too much decentralization leads to a fragmented product and a complex communication problem. Too little decentralization leads to workers with no line of sight to their customers, which tends to remove meaning from work.

Pixar is a good example of a wise decentralization strategy; it decentralized by movie. True, this resulted in teams of 200 to 250, slightly larger than Dunbar's Number of 150, but the structure kept software graphics experts tightly integrated with creative storytellers and artists, with everyone working toward a single goal: an awesome movie.

The goal of decentralization is to create interdisciplinary teams focused on market and customer needs, as opposed to teams focused

---

17. See especially Geoffrey A. Moore, *Escape Velocity: Free Your Company's Future from the Pull of the Past* (Harper Business, 2011).

on internal company competencies. When market-focused teams exist and have the leadership, the autonomy, the time, and the motivation, a good number of them can be expected to generate new ideas and then figure out how to transform those ideas into innovative new products, platforms, and services.

> **Anna:** How is decentralization different from outsourcing? **M&T:** Outsourcing generally means moving routine work to a lower-wage country; it usually does not imply that the outsourced location has autonomous multidisciplinary teams. However, that is not always the case. In the next section we will discuss a case in which a company expanded into India and China to escape the trap of traditional development processes while obtaining the advantage of a development team much closer to its target market.

Case: Harman[18]

Harman has been a leader in high-end automotive navigation and entertainment (infotainment) systems for many years; in fact, it owned 70% of the high-end infotainment system market in 2007. Obviously, you don't own 70% of a market unless you are very good. Make no mistake—the engineers at Harman were excellent.

But there wasn't much more space to expand in the high-end market, and Harman systems were too expensive for lower-priced cars. The problem was that demand for infotainment systems was growing in those lower-priced markets. The company wanted to enter the low-end market, but the first attempt at lowering the price of its system was pretty much a disaster. Harman's engineering teams were excellent in addressing the high-end market, but that expertise did not extend to low-priced products.

CEO Dinesh Paliwal asked Sachin Lawande, Chief Software Architect for Infotainment Systems, to lead an effort to develop a system that would sell for half the price and cost one-third as much as the existing system. Lawande came from the embedded software world, where the mantra was *Do more with less.* He was frustrated by the complexity of the current product line, which had to undergo expensive customization for each new sale. As an architect, he realized that

---

18. Information in this section is from Vijay Govindarajan and Chris Trimble, *Reverse Innovation: Create Far from Home, Win Everywhere* (Harvard Business Review Press, 2012), Chapter 9.

the new system would have to be modular, that customization would have to be accomplished by assembling a system out of standard modules. And he knew that the complex organizational structure currently in place was not conducive to building a simple, modular system. He would have to set up a separate organization.

Lawande hired a small software group in Bangalore, India, and a small hardware group in Suzhou, China. He added a few Harman engineers to lead and guide the new engineers. And then he formed development teams. They were not organized by discipline (hardware, software, etc.) or by location (China, India, Germany, etc.); they were organized by module. For example, the navigation team had people from various locations and disciplines who were jointly responsible for the navigation module. This violated the prevailing wisdom of most Harman engineers, who had worked in functional groups. It violated the advice of most agile consultants, who recommend colocated teams. But it worked.[19]

The Harman engineering organization was skeptical that the new product would succeed. But since Lawande reported to the CEO, he was able to proceed in his own way. Time was short, so Lawande limited the first product to the few features that customers of the high-end systems use all the time; additional features could be added later. He insisted that the system be built from standard chips. This led the team to discover that smartphone technology provided plenty of options—a cheap GPS chip, for instance. And he urged the teams to use open source software and off-the-shelf subsystems. So rather than develop a navigation system, they spent their limited time developing a module that allowed the system to integrate with any navigation device on the market.

In an amazingly short time—about a year—the product, called Saras (Sanskrit for "adaptable"), was launched. Success was not instant, however, because the larger company was deeply suspicious of this "cheap" product. Sales reps had to be ordered to sell it. Customers were invited to visit the Saras engineers in China and India to gain confidence in their capability. Finally, Toyota placed a large order, and salespeople discovered that selling a large number of small but profitable units was actually a pretty good deal. Sales took off, and within 18 months, Saras sales revenue approached that of the high-end infotainment products, and its margins were *higher*. The stock price of the company rose by a factor of four. Innovation, Saras-style, has become a core competency of the company.

---

19. The "right" organizational structure is a matter of context.

. . . From Product to Problem

 For 30 years, General Electric (GE) pursued a policy it called **glocalization**—products were perfected in the United States, Europe, and Japan and moved to the rest of the world. But CEO Jeffrey Immelt came to realize that the growth opportunities in key businesses such as power distribution and health care were located in China and India, where demand for these basics is on a nonlinear growth curve. However, the high-end products GE brought to power distribution and health care were far too expensive to use in rural areas where most of the growth will occur, and removing features was not going to solve this problem. It became apparent that products to serve these low-cost, high-demand markets had to be designed from the ground up.

However, the entire GE organizational structure, measurement systems, and culture were optimized around existing product lines. If the current practices were not dramatically altered, GE would never be able to address those growth markets, and someday the companies that did would be positioned to bring their products into GE's home territory. GE knew how to compete against its traditional rivals, but new competitors with a whole new price-performance paradigm would pose a formidable threat.

Case: GE Healthcare[20]

Almost by accident, an interesting organizational model arose in China that had a lot of potential. A GE research lab in Israel had found a way to move most of the functions typically performed in ultrasound hardware to software running on a PC; however, no one was interested in this capability, because it would probably cannibalize a line of products that sold for upward of $150,000. Then Omar Ishrak, an outsider with a lot of experience in ultrasound devices, was hired to lead GE's three ultrasound business areas. Ishrak felt that a low-cost ultrasound device would be an excellent product for China and realized that the typical GE organizational structure would squelch any local effort. So he created an independent local growth team (LGT) that had complete business responsibility for developing, manufacturing, and selling a PC-based ultrasound device suitable for rural Chinese clinics.

---

20. Information in this section is from Jeffrey R. Immelt, Vijay Govindarajan, and Chris Trimble, "How GE Is Disrupting Itself," *Harvard Business Review* 87, no. 10 (October 2009).

By 2002, the team was selling a $30,000 device; by 2007, the price had come down to $15,000; and in 2010 a $7,900 pocket-size ultrasound device was released. Even as sales in China grew rapidly, the new ultrasound device was introduced into U.S. and European markets for use where portability and rapid diagnosis are important—emergency rooms, hospital floors, ambulances—creating a whole new category of medical device. Today the product is a resounding success.

This is the classic tale of a disruptive innovation, and its success was attributed to the LGT concept, which is based on five key principles:

1. Shift power to where the growth is.
2. Build new offerings from the ground up.
3. Build LGTs from the ground up, like new companies.
4. Customize objectives, targets, and metrics.
5. Have the LGT report to someone high in the organization.

GE India Using the ultrasound LGT as a model, Immelt decided to make the entire country of India into a separate business unit reporting to a senior executive. This was not easy; it violated the prevailing wisdom in the company. GE had a matrix structure where product had always come before country, so managing a country as a separate business unit was "anathema." But Immelt realized that GE was structured and managed to support the glocalization strategy, and this strategy had to be changed. He used a country-focused organizational structure to drive the change.

Since GE's first interdisciplinary R&D center outside the United States was already established in Bangalore, GE India had its own product development capability. With its newly granted ability to make local decisions, GE India chose to focus on developing an electrocardiogram (ECG) device, since heart disease is the single largest cause of death in India. There was a real need for a low-cost, ultraportable ECG device that would allow rural health care professionals to diagnose the many people who could not travel to a city for an ECG.

Just as in China, the locally developed device was very different from anything available from the rest of GE, but it had all of the software power of any ECG device in the company. Because it was designed for rural India, it was especially easy to use and easy to repair; and because electricity is unreliable in rural India, it was operated by a battery with an exceptionally long life. These days, the lowest-cost GE device can be used to administer an ECG in almost any setting in rural India for about the price of a cup of tea.

Just as with the ultrasound device developed in China, India's ECG devices quickly made their way into more developed countries for use in situations where portability, low power, and low cost are important. Immelt's strategy of going local to create disruptive innovation was beginning to work.

Anna: As I recall, in Chapter 1 you mentioned that Alan Mulally's strategy at Ford was exactly the opposite—he centralized car designs and moved away from individual designs for each country.

M&T: You are right. And this proves that there is no one-size-fits-all innovation strategy. The "right" strategy depends on the industry, the company, and the current context. The idea is to keep the tiny signals of budding opportunities from being lost in the unavoidable noise of running a successful business.

An Innovation Checklist

If you want your company to survive over the long term, there is no substitute for creating an adaptable, innovative organization. Here is what that means in practice:

1. **Give product developers a clear line of sight to their customers.**

   Be careful that roles such as Product Manager or Product Owner are not implemented in a way that divorces developers from customers. This is a big mistake; it lengthens feedback loops and confines the creative power of developers to implementation issues.

2. **Form interdisciplinary teams.**

   Teams cannot be autonomous if they do not contain within them all of the skills necessary to understand and address customer problems.

   a. **Build respect across disciplines.**

      Interdisciplinary teams are not a magic potion that will solve all problems. Getting people in those various disciplines to understand and respect each other is a huge task.

b. **Check out your compensation system.**
Does your compensation system discourage teamwork through individual incentives? Does it discourage respect between disciplines through unequal compensation of different disciplines?

3. **Disrupt yourself.**

If you are in a high-tech field, you can count on disruptive technologies to threaten your core business every five to ten years. It would be better if you were the inventor of those disruptive businesses, but the only way to do so is to find simpler, cheaper ways to solve customer problems.

a. **Be skeptical of high prices.**
Consider Skype, which devastated a telecom industry that subsidized local service with high-cost long-distance service.

b. **Be skeptical of barriers to access content.**
Andy Grove wanted a law named after himself, and here is the law he proposed: "Technology always wins. You can delay technology by legal interference, but technology will flow around legal barriers."

c. **Be skeptical of your approach to allocating resources.**
GE found that its approach to allocating funds to development efforts was completely impenetrable for someone in India who had a good idea for a product that would serve rural needs at a low price. It took a change in organizational structure to allow innovation to happen at the local level.

4. **Change what you pay attention to.**

What you pay attention to sends signals to people about what's important.

a. **Stop worrying about productivity.**
Start worrying about doing the right thing; it's much more important.

b. **Create a process that encourages experiments.**
It can be 20% time, it can be regular hackathons, it can be internal venture funding for experiments—whatever process you choose, find a way to encourage teams to conduct quick experiments and expect a good number of them to fail.

   c. **Decouple your architecture.**

     Conway's Law[21] says the system architecture reflects corporate structure. If you want to decentralize your people, you will need to decentralize your architecture. Consider platforms built from services.

   d. **Walk in the shoes of your customers.**

     Innovative companies understand what frustrates and what delights their customers better than anyone else—even better than their customers.

   e. **Articulate a high-level purpose.**

     People do not put their heart and soul into increasing shareholder value.

5. **Develop support systems for innovation.**

Teams do not automatically know how to go about being innovative; they need training, coaching, leadership, time, and, most of all, the understanding that this is what the company expects them to do.

6. **Live in the future.**[22]

Create plausible future scenarios and imagine how you might deal with them.

   a. **Imagine a 5× change in some dimension of your business.**

     Imagine a product that costs five times less than your current best-selling product, that consumes one-fifth the power, and/or is one-fifth the size. What is the market for this product? What additional customers can you sell it to?

   b. **Imagine the technology landscape 15 years from now.**

     Think backward to what the technology landscape was 15 years ago. Then imagine the same amount of change over the next 15 years. What does this future look like? Where does your company fit into the picture?

---

21. In 1968, Melvin Conway wrote: "Organizations which design systems . . . are constrained to produce designs which are copies of the communication structures of these organizations." See our book *Leading Lean Software Development*, pp. 67–69.
22. See Angela Wilkinson and Roland Kupers, "Living in the Futures: How Scenario Planning Changed Corporate Strategy," *Harvard Business Review*, May 2013.

c. **Imagine the workplace at your company 20 years from now.**
Imagine what your company's workplace will be like when today's teenagers form the core of the workforce and provide
most of the management.

Questions to Ponder

1. Imagine that a new CEO came in to run your business. What is
the first thing that person would do?

2. Imagine that you are asked to redesign your core product from
scratch for today's markets using today's technology. What does
it look like?

3. Imagine that your best outsourcing partner started designing products for its local area instead of working under contract to your
company. What kind of products would the company design?

4. Imagine that it is five years from now and your core product is
no longer very popular or profitable. What happened? How do
your (former) customers do the job they were doing with your
product?

5. Compare the metrics for one of your ongoing business units to
the metrics that a venture capital firm would apply to a startup
company. How do they differ?

6. Does your company have strategies in place to combat confirmation bias (the tendency to seek out or interpret information in
a way that will confirm preexisting viewpoints)? What are they?
How well do they work?

7. Which jobs on a product team are "high status"? Which are "low
status"? How well do people from the two different areas interact with each other?

8. Is there a stigma attached to people who work on a creative new
venture that fails—in your company's culture? In your country's
culture?

9. What does productivity mean in your company? How do
you measure it? How is it related to your company's overall
performance?

10. What does predictability mean in your company? Is it important? Why?

Epilogue

We have traveled to many countries since we finished this book: Australia, China, England, Estonia, Germany, India, Ireland, Japan, Latvia, New Zealand, Norway, Sweden, Vietnam—as well as our own USA. In location after location, we have found that agile development has been widely adopted in the software world. And generally speaking, the results have been positive: higher-quality software is being delivered to customers quite a bit faster than before.

But there is a problem. Many customers are underwhelmed; agile methods often fail to deliver significantly improved business results. And many agile development team members are underwhelmed as well. Agile practices are usually not thought of as engaging and challenging—it's difficult to get inspired by a prioritized list of stories.

As we traveled around the world, we heard the same refrain many times: *We've adopted agile and it's a step in the right direction, but it is not enough. So* (we were asked repeatedly) *what's next?*

What's next is to stop thinking about software development as a delivery process and to start thinking of it as a problem-solving process, a creative process. Time and again we run into software delivery organizations—IT departments operating as cost centers and software firms working under contract—whose job is to turn someone else's requirements into delivered software. Agile practices have helped these organizations handle requirements in smaller batches, reduce work-in-progress, and speed up software delivery. But unfortunately, agile practices do not address the underlying problem: the very idea of a software delivery organization is flawed.

The concept of a software delivery organization is so ingrained in the structure of many companies that questioning its existence is nearly impossible. Yet there are many companies—typically those founded after the mid-1990s—that never got around to creating software delivery organizations in the first place. These companies purchase digital infrastructure as a commodity and consider the development of software-intensive products to be a line responsibility. They don't think of software as something to be delivered; they think of it as one of the raw materials that goes into a product. Consequently, they do not have software delivery teams; they have product development teams.

What is the difference between product development teams and software delivery teams? The most important difference is that product development team members find it easier to become engaged in their work. Rather than implementing lists of requirements, they are expected to think creatively, solve problems, and make trade-offs based on things such as profitability, market share, and long-term business impact. The sense of purpose, the challenge, and the local decision making found on product teams bring out the best in people.

Product teams are judged by the business results they produce rather than by proxy measures such as cost, schedule, and scope. Therefore, product teams include everyone involved in the end-to-end feedback loop from problem to solution. Given the proper charter and appropriate staffing, it is common for product teams to uncover and solve hidden problems, change course quickly, and take advantage of unexpected opportunities. Consequently, product teams tend to be good at delivering superior business results.

Delivery teams operate under a significant handicap. They are chartered to implement someone else's solutions to problems that team members are not expected to understand. They deliver these solutions without assuming responsibility—or receiving credit—for the resulting business improvements. Even when agile practices speed up delivery, feedback loops are lengthy and plagued with handovers. Therefore, it is a challenge for delivery teams to find a purpose, generate enthusiasm, or spark innovation. So it should not be a surprise when these teams deliver mediocre business results.

Why are software delivery organizations so common despite the obvious handicaps? Historically, digital technology has been outside the competence of most company founders and line business leaders, so creating a separate organization to manage this mysterious technology seemed logical. But in a world where virtually all leaders grow up immersed in digital technology and most offerings depend on software, such segregation makes less sense.

A second reason for separating software development from other parts of the enterprise is the assumption that a standard technical approach at the enterprise level leads to greater overall efficiency, and for many decades this may have been true. But with the commoditization of enterprise infrastructure and the coming of age of architectures built on decoupled services, this rationale is becoming obsolete.

A third reason for separate delivery organizations stems from the strong influence of Adam Smith's division of labor theory on Western cultures. We are conditioned to believe that the most efficient way to get things done is to decompose work into its component parts and assign each component to a specialist. Of course, efficiency also demands that each specialist be kept busy, so as not to waste valuable time.

When work can be broken down into clear segments of predictable effort, assigning work to specialists and keeping them fully occupied is one path to efficiency. But development—the discovery and validation of effective solutions to important problems—is not supposed to be predictable; it is supposed to be exploratory, creative, and responsive to feedback. Product development excellence is the result of constant, bidirectional communication among specialties. In such an environment, the path to efficiency is not *resource efficiency*—keeping specialists busy. For developing new ideas, the path to genuine efficiency is *flow efficiency*—moving ideas from concept to cash (or trash) with as little delay as possible.

Flow efficiency is easiest to achieve with organizational structures that are orthogonal to those optimized for resource efficiency. Instead of departments formed around specialties such as software development, we find departments organized around the units that flow through the organization. Flow-efficient hospitals are organized around patients as they move through stages of care. Flow-efficient factories are organized around customer orders as they move through stages of manufacturing. Flow-efficient development is organized around product concepts as they move from inception to commercialization.

Software delivery organizations were born in an age when a focus on resource efficiency was considered common sense. But that kind of common sense is obsolete. The islands of efficiency created by resource-efficient mindsets have become islands of inefficiency in today's world. The pace of market change demands a shift to flow efficiency, and modern digital technologies provide the necessary support. It's time to drain the lake that separates specialties into islands that communicate via boatloads of documents. It's time to create a new terrain, one where software is just another aspect of an integrated landscape.

We have spent a lot of time over the past decade working to make life better for those who develop software. We promote lean principles such as small batches and steady flow and quality at the source. Over the past few years we have watched the waters recede and marveled as islands of software development became part of the mainland. We have observed that the best and brightest software specialists have learned to talk directly with customers, work as partners with other disciplines, and seek out new approaches to solving problems.

We have written three books about software development, but we couldn't write a fourth, because the islands of software development have largely disappeared. In their place we find a new landscape, one in which infrastructure is a commodity and multidiscipline teams are expected to ask the right questions, solve the right problems, and deliver solutions that customers love. True, those solutions are often software-intensive. In fact, just about everything is software-intensive these days, so isolating software on its own island doesn't make much sense anymore.

This is a book about thriving in the new landscape, a land without islands, a land that is a bit short of specialists, a land that's full of endless possibilities.

References

ABC *Nightline,* "IDEO Designing a Shopping Cart." www.youtube.com/watch?v=M66ZU2PCIcM.

Adner, Ron. *The Wide Lens: A New Strategy for Innovation.* New York: Penguin Publishing, 2012.

Adzic, Gojko. *Impact Mapping.* Woking, UK: Provoking Thoughts, 2012.

Amabile, Teresa, and Steven Kramer. *The Progress Principle: Using Small Wins to Ignite Joy, Engagement, and Creativity at Work.* Boston: Harvard Business Review Press, 2011.

Amabile, Teresa M., and Steven J. Kramer. "What Really Motivates Workers." In "The HBR List: Breakthrough Ideas for 2010," *Harvard Business Review,* January 2010.

Amazon.com. Amazon Corporate Governance Message. http://phx.corporate-ir.net/phoenix.zhtml?c=97664&p=irol-govHighlights.

Ariely, Dan. *Predictably Irrational: The Hidden Forces That Shape Our Decisions.* New York: HarperCollins, 2010.

Bamber, Greg J., Jody Hoffer Gittell, Thomas A. Kochan, and Andrew von Nordenflycht. "Up in the Air: How Airlines Can Improve Performance by Engaging Their Employees," *Newsweek,* February 5, 2010, especially pp. 87–96.

Benioff, Marc, and Eric Schmidt. Dreamforce 2011, September 5, 2011. www.youtube.com/watch?v=JDl5hb0XbfY.

Benkler, Yochai. "The Unselfish Gene," *Harvard Business Review,* July–August 2011.

———. Keynote talk at LSSC2012, "The Penguin the Leviathan: Cooperative Human Systems Design," Boston, May 16, 2012. http://vimeo.com/channels/339107/page:8.

Blackwell, Lisa, Kali Trzesniewski, and Carol Dweck. "Implicit Theories of Intelligence Predict Achievement across an Adolescent Transition: A Longitudinal Study and an Intervention," *Child Development* 78, no. 1 (January–February 2007): 246–63.

Boehm, Barry. *Software Engineering Economics.* Englewood Cliffs, NJ: Prentice Hall, 1981.

Bower, Joseph and Clayton Christensen. "Disruptive Technologies: Catching the Wave," *Harvard Business Review,* January, 1995.

Carr, Austin. "Intuit Taps Text Messages, Economics to Boost Farmer Incomes in India," *Fast Company.* www.fastcoexist.com/1679081/intuit-taps-text-messages-economics-to-boost-farmer-incomes-in-india.

Catmull, Ed. "How Pixar Fosters Collective Creativity," *Harvard Business Review* 86, no. 9 (September 2008).

Christensen, Clayton. *The Innovator's Dilemma.* Boston: Harvard Business School Press, 1997.

Cohan, Peter. "Can Scott Cook Revive Corporate America?" *Forbes,* February 29, 2012. www.forbes.com/sites/petercohan/2012/02/29/can-scott-cook-revive-corporate-america/.

Collins, Jim, and Jerry I. Porras. *Built to Last: Successful Habits of Visionary Companies.* New York: Harper Business, 2004.

Comstock, Beth, and Eric Ries. "Lean Startup 2012" video. www.youtube.com/watch?v=TW96_fCSFiU&list=UUQnF0c8GaWDm9T4yMDpGcPA&index=25.

Crouch, Tom. "Tom Crouch Talks Wright Brothers," August 19, 2007. http://wrightstories.com/tom-crouch-talks-wright-brothers/.

Csikszentmihalyi, Mihaly. *Flow: The Psychology of Optimal Experience.* New York: HarperCollins, 1990.

Dietz, Doug. "Transforming Healthcare for Children and Their Families," TEDxSanJoseCA 2012. www.youtube.com/watch?v=jajduxPD6H4.

Downes, Larry, and Paul Nunes. "Big-Bang Disruption," *Harvard Business Review,* March 2013.

Drucker, Peter. *Management: Tasks, Responsibilities, Practices.* New York: Harper & Row, 1974.

Drucker, Peter F. "What We Can Learn from Japanese Management," *Harvard Business Review,* March–April 1971.

Dunbar, Robin. *How Many Friends Does One Person Need?* Cambridge, MA: Harvard University Press, 2010.

Dweck, Carol. *Mindset: The New Psychology of Success.* New York: Random House, 2006.

Escalante, Jaime, and Jack Dirmann. "The Jaime Escalante Math Program," *Journal of Negro Education* 59, no. 3 (Summer 1990): 407–23.

Financial Times. "Welch Condemns Share Price Focus," March 12, 2009. www.ft.com/intl/cms/s/0/294ff1f2-0f27-11de-ba10-0000779fd2ac. html#axzz2EyBD8eJ2.

Fox, Justin, and Jay W. Lorsch. "What Good Are Shareholders?" *Harvard Business Review,* July–August 2012.

Frey, B. S., and R. Jegen. "Motivation Crowding Theory," *Journal of Economic Surveys* 15, no. 5 (2001): 589–611.

Gilb, Tom. *Principles of Software Engineering Management.* London: Pearson Education, 1988.

———. "Value-Driven Development Principles and Values," *Agile Record,* July 2010.

Gladwell, Malcolm. *Tipping Point: How Little Things Can Make a Big Difference.* Little, Brown and Company, 2002.

Google. Google Investor Relations 2004 Founders IPO Letter. http://investor .google.com/corporate/2004/ipo-founders-letter.html.

Govindarajan, Vijay, and Chris Trimble. *Reverse Innovation: Create Far from Home, Win Everywhere.* Boston: Harvard Business Review Press, 2012.

Grove, Andrew S. *Only the Paranoid Survive: How to Exploit the Crisis Points That Challenge Every Company.* New York: Doubleday Business, 1996.

Grove, Andy. "Andy Grove: How America Can Create Jobs," *Bloomburg Business Week,* July 1, 2010.

Halvorson, Heidi Grant. *Succeed: How We Can Reach Our Goals.* New York: Hudson Street Press, 2010.

Harford, Tim. *Adapt: Why Success Always Starts with Failure.* New York: Picador, 2012.

Heath, Chip, and Dan Heath. *Decisive: How to Make Better Choices in Life and Work.* New York: Crown Business, 2013.

Heine, Steven J., et al. "Divergent Consequences of Success and Failure in Japan and North America: An Investigation of Self-Improving Motivations and Malleable Selves," *Journal of Personality and Social Psychology* 81, no. 4 (2001): 599–615.

Higgins, E. Tory. "Beyond Pleasure and Pain," *American Psychologist,* December 1977.

Hoffman, Bryce G. *American Icon: Alan Mulally and the Fight to Save Ford Motor Company.* New York: Crown Business, 2012.

Humble, Jez, and Dave Farley. *Continuous Delivery.* Boston: Addison-Wesley, 2010.

Immelt, Jeffrey R., Vijay Govindarajan, and Chris Trimble. "How GE Is Disrupting Itself," *Harvard Business Review* 87, no. 10 (October 2009).

Israel, Jerome. "Why the FBI Can't Build a Case Management System," *IEEE Computer* 45, no. 6 (June 2012).

Jensen, Michael C., and William H. Meckling. "Theory of the Firm: Managerial Behavior, Agency Costs and Ownership Structure," *Journal of Financial Economics,* October 1976.

Kadaba, Bharath. "Improving Earning Capacity of Farmers: Case Study by One World Foundation India." www.ustream.tv/recorded/27482093/highlight/311462/theater.

———. Talk at Lean Startup Conference, San Francisco, December 4, 2012. www.ustream.tv/recorded/27482093/highlight/311462/theater.

Kahneman, Daniel. *Thinking, Fast and Slow.* New York and London: Farrar, Straus and Giroux, 2011.

Kahneman, Daniel, and Gary Klein. "Conditions for Intuitive Expertise: A Failure to Disagree," *American Psychologist* 64, no. 6 (September 2009): 515–26.

Kanter, Rosabeth Moss. "How Great Companies Think Differently," *Harvard Business Review,* November 2011.

Kennedy, Michael, and Kent Harmon. *Ready, Set, Dominate.* Richmond, VA: Oaklea Press, 2008. See also www.targetedconvergence.com.

Keshava, Jagannath, Nagib Hakim, and Chinna Prudvi. "Post-Silicon Validation Challenges: How EDA and Academia Can Help," presented at DAC '10, Anaheim, CA, 2010. http://dl.acm.org/citation.cfm?id=1837278&dl=ACM&coll=DL&CFID=321233734&CFTOKEN=43954004.

Klein, Gary. *Sources of Power: How People Make Decisions.* Cambridge, MA: The MIT Press, 1998.

———. *Streetlights and Shadows: Searching for the Keys to Adaptive Decision Making.* Cambridge, MA: The MIT Press, 2009.

Kniberg, Henrik. "Scaling Agile @ Spotify with Tribes, Squads, Chapters, and Guilds," 2012. http://blog.crisp.se/2012/11/14/henrikkniberg/scaling-agile-at-spotify.

Koeppen, Brynn. "Todd Park on Entrepreneurship, Mobility and 'Health Datapalooza.'" In "Execs to Know, Information Tech, Mobility, Small Business," January 4, 2012. www.washingtonexec.com/2012/01/todd-park-on-entrepreneurship-mobility-and-health-datapalooza/.

Kollock, Peter. "The Economies of Online Cooperation: Gifts and Public Goods in Cyberspace." In *Communities in Cyberspace,* edited by Marc A. Smith and Peter Kollock, pp. 219–40. London and New York: Routledge, 1999.

Lafley, A. G., Roger L. Martin, Jan W. Rivkin, and Nicolaj Siggelkow. "Bringing Science to the Art of Strategy," *Harvard Business Review,* September 2012.

Levitt, Theodore. "Marketing Myopia," *Harvard Business Review,* July–August 1960.

Liedtka, Jeanne, and Tim Ogilvie. *Designing for Growth.* New York: Columbia University Press, 2011.

Lilienthal, Otto. *Birdflight as the Basis of Aviation.* Published in German in 1889. In English: Hummelstown, PA: Markowski International, 2000.

Limoncelli, Tom, Jesse Robbins, Kripa Krishnan, and John Allspaw. "Resilience Engineering: Learning to Embrace Failure," *Communications of the ACM,* November 2012.

Martin, Roger. "The Age of Customer Capitalism," *Harvard Business Review,* January–February 2010.

Merchant, Nilofer. *The New How: Building Business Solutions through Collaborative Strategy.* North Sebastopol, CA: O'Reilly Media, 2009.

Miller, Dale T. "The Norm of Self-Interest," *American Psychologist,* December 1999.

Modig, Niklas, and Par Ahlstrom. *This Is Lean: Resolving the Efficiency Paradox.* Stockholm: Rheologica Publishing, 2012.

Moore, Geoffrey A. *Escape Velocity: Free Your Company's Future from the Pull of the Past.* New York: Harper Business, 2011.

Moore, Gordon. Intel Developer Forum Keynote. www.intel.com/pressroom/archive/speeches/gem93097.htm.

One World Foundation India. "Improving Earning Capacity of Farmer," http://indiagovernance.gov.in/files/intuit_fasal_edited_intuit_final.pdf.

Ostrom, Elinor. *Governing the Commons: The Evolution of Institutions for Collective Action.* New York: Cambridge University Press, 1990.

Owens, Simon. "Can Todd Park Revolutionize the Health Care Industry?" *Atlantic,* June 2011. www.theatlantic.com/technology/archive/2011/06/can-todd-park-revolutionize-the-health-care-industry/239708/.

Park, Todd. Talk at TechCrunch Disrupt, 2012. http://techcrunch.com/2012/05/23/us-cto-todd-park-obama-has-a-very-high-geek-quotient-but-its-all-a-means-to-an-end/.

Perry, Mark J. "Carpe Diem," Blog for Economics and Finance, October 5, 2012. http://mjperry.blogspot.com/2012/09/freefall-adjusted-for-inflation-print.html.

Pfeffer, Jeffrey. "Lay Off the Layoffs," *Newsweek,* February 5, 2010.

———. "Shareholders First? Not So Fast . . . ," *Harvard Business Review,* August 2009.

Pfeffer, Jeffrey, and Robert Sutton. "Evidence-Based Management," *Harvard Business Review,* January 2006.

Poppendieck, Mary, and Tom Poppendieck. *Leading Lean Software Development*. Boston: Addison-Wesley, 2010.

Preston, Rob. "General Motors Will Slash Outsourcing in IT Overhaul," *InformationWeek*, July 9, 2012.

Raynor, Michael, and Mumtaz Ahmed. "Three Rules for Making a Company Truly Great," *Harvard Business Review*, April 2013.

Reichheld, Fred. *The Ultimate Question 2.0*. Boston: Harvard Business Review Press, 2011.

Ries, Eric. *The Lean Startup: How Today's Entrepreneurs Use Continuous Innovation to Create Radically Successful Businesses*. New York: Crown Business, 2011.

Sampson, Robert J. *Great American City: Chicago and the Enduring Neighborhood Effect*. Chicago: The University of Chicago Press, 2012.

Seddon, John. *Freedom from Command and Control: Rethinking Management for Lean Service*. New York: Productivity Press, 2005.

Spector, Alfred, Peter Norvig, and Slav Petrov. "Google's Hybrid Approach to Research," *Communications of the ACM* 55, no. 7 (July 2012).

Stanovich, K. E. *Who Is Rational? Studies of Individual Differences in Reasoning*. Mahwah, NJ: Lawrence Erlbaum Associates, 1999.

Stanovich, K. E., and R. F. West. "Individual Differences in Reasoning: Implications for the Rationality Debate," *Behav. Brain Sci.* 23 (2000): 645–726.

Thomke, Stefan, and Donald Reinertsen. "Six Myths of Product Development," *Harvard Business Review*, May 2012.

Ton, Zeynep. "Why 'Good Jobs' Are Good for Retailers," *Harvard Business Review*, January–February 2013.

Vogels, Werner. "Working Backwards." www.allthingsdistributed.com/2006/11/working_backwards.html.

Wilkinson, Angela, and Roland Kupers. "Living in the Futures: How Scenario Planning Changed Corporate Strategy," *Harvard Business Review*, May 2013.

Wright, Orville. *How We Invented the Airplane: An Illustrated History*, edited by Fred C. Kelly. First published in 1953 from text written in 1920. Republished with new material in 1988 by Dover Publications, Inc.

Index